DOONESBURY

A Musical Comedy

DOONESBURY

A Musical Comedy

Book and Lyrics by G. B. Trudeau

Music by Elizabeth Swados

AN OWL BOOK · HOLT, RINEHART AND WINSTON · New York

Published by Holt, Rinehart and Winston,
383 Madison Avenue, New York, New York 10017.
Published simultaneously in Canada by Holt, Rinehart and
Winston of Canada, Limited.

LC: 84-756267
ISBN: 0-03-000503-5

First Edition

Designer: Robert Bull

Printed in the United States of America

10 9 8 7 6 5 4 3 2 1

ISBN 0-03-000503-5

DOONESBURY

A Musical Comedy

Book and Lyrics by G. B. Trudeau
Music by Elizabeth Swados
Cast
(in order of appearance)

ROLAND	Reathel Bean
MIKE DOONESBURY	Ralph Bruneau
MARK	Mark Linn-Baker
B.D.	Keith Szarabajka
BOOPSIE	Laura Dean
ZONKER	Albert Macklin
DUKE	Gary Beach
HONEY	Lauren Tom
J.J.	Kate Burton
JOANIE	Barbara Andres

Produced by James Walsh
In Association with Universal Pictures
Directed by Jacques Levy
Choreography by Margo Sappington
Scenery Designed by Peter Larkin
Costumes Designed by Patricia McGourty
Lighting Designed by Beverly Emmons
Sound Designed by Tom Morse

Based on "Doonesbury" by G. B. Trudeau by permission of
Universal Press Syndicate.

First performed at the Biltmore Theater in New York on
November 21, 1983.

Original cast album available from MCA Records.

ACT ONE
SCENE 1

We see a scrim of the White House. A press conference is in progress.

REPORTERS (*voice-over*): Mr. President! Mr. President!

REAGAN (*voice-over*): Yes, Helen.

HELEN (*voice-over*): Sir, your tuition tax credit program means, in effect, that parents who don't use the public school system won't have to support it. By that logic, shouldn't taxpayers who choose not to be defended by MX missiles also get tax credits?

REAGAN (*voice-over*): Uh . . . well, Helen, you've thrown me kind of a brainteaser there. Basically, I feel government should get out of education altogether. Take the student-loan program. In 1979, the average college student cost the taxpayers—

SAM (*voice-over*): Excuse me, Mr. President . . .

REAGAN (*voice-over*): Yes, Sam?

SAM (*voice-over*): Sir, as you know, you've already made twelve misstatements during this press conference, for a career total of 1,983. Should you get your facts wrong on this final answer, you will break your old record set last January 19th.

REAGAN (*voice-over*): Oh . . . um . . . okay. The average college student cost the government . . . um . . .

SAM (*voice-over*): Take your time, sir. This is the big one.

REAGAN (*voice-over*): You know, Sam, there's a reason for these tax credits. Sure, they benefit the well-to-do, but from past experience we know that they are the only class that can be depended on to put their tax cuts into savings and investments.

SAM (*voice-over*): And the poor?

REAGAN (*voice-over*): Studies show they tend to blow it all at the track.

The White House scrim is raised, revealing the living room of Walden Commune. Seated in a swivel chair in front of the television is MIKE. MARK *is sprawled out on a couch in the center of the room. Seated directly behind the television,* ROLAND, *resplendent in full news correspondent regalia, is delivering a report to an attentive* MIKE.

ROLAND: This is Roland Hedley. Who is today's college student? What manner of men and women attend our institutions of higher learning? An uncommon breed, caught in the cross hairs of history, they've set their sights high, only to see them dashed on deaf ears. Students say they can almost taste the fear. Why? Raging statistics, of course. Skyrocketing developments. Spiraling indicators. And yet these gathering storm clouds are just the tip of the iceberg. Be with me tomorrow as we watch some actual students graduate from college live.

MARK *looks up from the magazine he's been reading.*

MARK: Actual students? My God, Mike. He thinks we are actual students?

MIKE: Ssshh.

ROLAND: Whether or not they can scale the wall of indifference they face today remains to be seen, but one thing is clear: Life goes on.

MARK: No shit.

MIKE: Oh, that's so true.

ROLAND: This is Roland Hedley. I'll be back with some final comments after this. Peter?

PETER (*voice-over*): Thanks, Roland.

MARK: Mike?

MIKE: Mark?

At this moment, B.D. *enters from his bedroom,* BOOPSIE *closely in tow.*

MARK: Back to you, Mike.

MIKE: Thanks, Mark. Over to you, B.D.

B.D.: I don't want it.

MIKE: Boopsie?

BOOPSIE: What do I do with it?

MIKE: Throw it to Zonker.

BOOPSIE: Zonker!

ZONKER *sticks his head out of his bedroom door.*

ZONKER: What?

BOOPSIE (*to* ZONKER): Good-night from all of us.

ZONKER: Thanks, Boopsie. I'll be back in a moment. Mark?

ZONKER *disappears back into his room. The musical intro to "Graduation" begins.*

MARK: Thanks, Zonker. Now this.

MIKE (*sings*):
That's the view here.

MARK (*sings*):
For the time being.

BOOPSIE (*sings*):
Back to you, Dan.

MIKE (*sings*):
All that's clear, Ted.

MARK (*sings*):
Remains to be seen.

B.D. (*sings*):
Throw it to Sam, man.

BOOPSIE (*sings*):
Whether or not, Tom,
This outlook survives.

MARK, MIKE, B.D., BOOPSIE (*sing*):
Time will tell what
We do with our lives.

ALL (*sing*):
  Graduation
  Will probably stand
  The test of time
  And it's almost at hand.
  Whether we sort
  The pros from the con,
  Time will tell
  If life will go on.

MARK (*shouting*): Hey, Zonker! You're missing Roland's story on students.

ZONKER *looks out his door again.*

ZONKER: I am?

MARK: Yup.

ZONKER: Oh, dear. What's the state of the student so far?

MARK: Well, he's out of sorts, but not dangerous.

  Reassured, ZONKER *enters.*

ZONKER (*sings*):
  Oh, it gives a student pause,
  When his teachers pass him without cause.
  They have tenure, why can't we?
  The Real World chews up kids like me.
  Could I slip into the office of the dean,
  Break into his files with a knife,
  Wipe my record clean,
  Make myself a freshman . . . for life?
  How could this have happened to me?
  No one failed more scrupulously.
  I've been double-crossed.
  Can't they see what's lost?
  The tragic, human cost . . . of . . .

ALL (*sing*):
  Graduation
  Will probably stand
  The test of time
  And it's almost at hand.

Whether we sort
The pros from the con,
Time will tell
If life will go on.

B.D.: Isn't it amazing which of us turned out to be the only one to actually graduate with a profession?

MARK: A profession? Please.

B.D.: Professional football isn't a profession?

ZONKER: Football? What do you mean, football? I thought you said you'd been drafted.

EVERYONE *stares at* ZONKER *in wonder.* ZONKER *slowly puts it together.*

ZONKER (*amazed*): My God. They can actually draft you to play football?

MIKE: Pretty scary, huh?

B.D.: Well, it sure as hell beats jacking off in B school.

ZONKER *laughs, as* MIKE *turns to the audience.*

MIKE (*sings*):
Business school is a very sensible choice,
I can take more time to find my individual voice.
Keep my illusions safely abstract,
Cruise through the news with my views intact,
Observe life as it passes me,
Interpret things historically,
And question them rhetorically,
And join the world while saving face,
We all can't have amazing grace.
Oh, business school is a very sensible choice
For me.

ALL (*sing*):
Graduation, Gra . . . Graduation!
Graduation, Gra . . . Graduation!
Graduation, Grad . . . Graduation!
Graduation.

ROLAND: Strange as it sounds.

ALL (*sing*):
  Will probably stand

ROLAND: Caps, tassels, and gowns

ALL (*sing*):
  The test of time . . .

ROLAND: The climate has wrought . . .

ALL (*sing*):
  And it's almost at hand.

ROLAND: A future that's fraught . . .

ALL (*sing*):
  Whether we sort . . .

ROLAND: With gathering gloom . . .

ALL (*sing*):
  The pros from the con . . .

ROLAND: Say prophets of doom . . .

ALL (*sing*):
  Time will tell . . .

ROLAND: When we resume.

ALL (*sing*):
  If life will go on.
  Graduation
    (Strange as it seems)
  Will probably stand
    (The end of our dreams)
  The test of time
    (Dreams we forsake)
  And it's almost at hand.
    (To go on the make)
  Whether we sort
    (Go with the flow)
  The pros from the con,
    (Win, place, or show)
  Time will tell
  If life will go on.

When the song ends, B.D. *and* BOOPSIE *exit, and the others flop down onto the couch.*

PETER (*voice-over*): Back to you, Roland.

ROLAND: Thanks, Peter. That's all for now. Be with us later tonight when ABC's ".30-.30" will present the latest developments in the bizarre Hollywood cocaine trial of former U.S. Ambassador Duke. That's tonight, 10:00 Eastern time, 9:00 Central time, right here on ABC Wide—

MIKE *turns the television off.*

MIKE: Hear that, Zonk? They're doing a whole special on your uncle's trial.

ZONKER: Yeah. I'm afraid Uncle Duke's in way over his head this time. If you ask me, he should have just skipped bail and split for Europe while he had the chance.

MARK *looks up suddenly.*

MARK: Oh, no.

ZONKER: What?

MARK: Oh, no!

ZONKER: What oh no?

MARK: You know what we forgot to do? You know what we completely forgot to do while we were college students?

ZONKER: What?

MARK: We forgot to go to Europe. We completely forgot to go to Europe and buy Eurailpasses and sew patches on our knapsacks and stay in filthy two-dollar youth hostels and get drunk at all of Hemingway's favorite cafés.

ZONKER: My God. You're right.

MARK: Dammit, Zonk, we can't let our early manhoods slip away like this. Let's go. Let's go to Europe.

ZONKER: Right now? I've got stuff in the dryer.

MARK: No, after graduation. We'll just pack up and split for Europe for the year.

ZONKER: Could we go to Turkey, too? I've always wanted to go through Turkish customs.

MARK: Fine with me.

ZONKER: Say, Mike, could you keep an eye on my plants? Also, there's a leak in the john. Call Mrs. Kirby and have her send—

MIKE *finally looks up.*

MIKE: Zonker, what are you talking about?

ZONKER: The house, of course. We'd like you to keep an eye on the house while we come of age in Europe and Asia Minor.

MIKE: Zonker, how am I going to do that? We're losing the house.

ZONKER: What do you mean, losing the house?

MIKE: Our lease runs out tomorrow. We have to vacate.

ZONKER: Pshaw. We'll just renew it.

MIKE: Zonker, you couldn't afford to stay even if we did get it renewed. You guys don't have jobs.

ZONKER: That's a vicious lie. Mark's radio station might put him on salary any day, and I'm doing a very respectable business with returnable bottles.

MIKE: Some jobs.

ZONKER: Well, excuse us, Mr. Fast Track!

MIKE: Zonker, you've got to face reality—

ZONKER *holds up his hands.*

ZONKER: Mike, Mike, Mike. Friend of friends. You're obviously not yourself today. And hey, why should you be? You're about to graduate. This is not the time to be making emotional decisions. Why don't we just sleep on it, and we can discuss it in the morning. Okay? Great.

MIKE: No, Zonker . . . Zonker!

ZONKER *exits out the front door.*

MARK: Hey, Mike, what's the problem here? This place is our home.

MIKE: Yeah, I know. Believe me, Mark, I don't want to leave Walden any more than you do. It's just that . . . well, things have changed. In a few weeks, I might . . . might . . .

MARK: Might what?

MIKE: I might be married.

MARK: Well, yes, there's always that possibility . . . Jesus, you're serious. Who? J.J.?

MIKE: Of course J.J.

MARK: When?

MIKE: Well, I'm not sure about the timing. I'm still working on my proposal.

MARK: That's what you've been working on for the last month? I thought it was a grant application.

MIKE: I've done three rough drafts. I'm on the polish now. (MIKE *hands* MARK *the draft of his proposal.*) Tell me if you think the tone of my opening is right.

MARK (*reads*): "Hi, J.J.? It's me, Mike." Jesus, Mike, she knows who you are. You don't have to identify yourself.

MIKE *reaches over and scratches out the offending sentence.*

MIKE: You're right. Nice catch. I'm glad you're checking this.

MARK (*resumes reading*): "J.J., you're probably going to think this is a really dumb idea . . ."

MIKE: It's a bit defensive, I know, but this way, if it blows up in my face, I can just turn the whole thing into a joke. On the other hand, if she starts to show some real interest, I just skip ahead to Section B.

MARK: Mike, are you sure you're ready for this?

MIKE: Of course.

MARK: Mike, if you were really ready for marriage, would you need a script?

MIKE: Of course.

MARK *hands* MIKE's *pad back to him and sits down.*

MARK: Mikey, Mikey, Mikey. Look, let's face it, the reason you're so nervous is that you don't really know J.J. all that well. Hell, you've probably never even slept with her, right?

MIKE: Slept with her? Hey, come on, Marcus! (MIKE *laughs a bit too loudly.*) Me? Slept with her? Hey, Mark, it's me, Mikey. Mike the Man. Mike tie-on-the-doorknob Doonesbury. (*A beat.*) You really think it's important?

MARK: You don't?

MIKE: Well, I'm not so sure, Mark. I don't see how one night would change anything. I mean, you never really know everything about a person anyway, do you? (*Sings.*)

Sure, she has secrets,
And private places,
Flights of fancy all alone.
She has disguises,
And hidden graces,
I have a few of my own.
Why try to solve each mystery in her eyes?
Why try to fill a jar with fireflies in
Just one night?
I have so many other nights ahead of me.
It's just one night,
I need more time to learn how it's supposed to be.
I'm trying to keep from soaring like a kite.
I'll be late,
I can wait,
For just one night.
Just one night,
It's not as if I never had a past with her.
It's just one night,
I must be careful not to go too fast with her.
I know we're new at learning how to care,
But if she
Comes to me
A night that's sweet and silvery,
I'll know that I was right,
Love is more
Than something for
Just one night.

SCENE 2

Walden Commune. Back Porch. Day. ZONKER *is on the back porch misting his plants—*ARNOLD, GINGER, RALPHIE, *and* LAURA.

ZONKER (*to* RALPHIE): Say when.

RALPHIE: When. Now the other side.

ZONKER: I just did the other side, Ralphie. It just hasn't soaked in yet.

RALPHIE: Oh.

ARNOLD: So when are your parents due in, Zonk?

ZONKER: I'm afraid they're not coming, big fellah. They just don't trust me anymore. They've already come back to see me graduate twice.

ARNOLD: Oh. Well, what about your Uncle Duke?

ZONKER: He's not coming, either, Arnold. He couldn't make bail.

GINGER: What a shame. I was so looking forward to meeting your family.

RALPHIE: Don't worry, Ginger. You can meet them after we get out to California.

ZONKER: California? Who said anything about California?

RALPHIE: Uh . . . well, nobody, I guess. I just assumed you'd be going home after graduation.

ZONKER: Sorry, Ralphie, we're staying on here.

LAURA: But what about your tanning career, Zonker? You know the California sun's the finest in the world.

ZONKER: Laura, you know I'm not on the tanning circuit anymore. I've retired.

All the PLANTS *laugh.*

ARNOLD: The Sultan of Suntans? Count Coppertone? Retired? Please.

ZONKER: I mean it, Arnold. Those days are behind me. Tanning is a young man's sport.

GINGER: Come on, Zonker, what else can you do? Pro tanning's been your life.

ZONKER: Yeah, I know. But that was a long time ago, Ginger. Back when my skin was soft and competitive. (*Sings*.)

> Hard to believe,
> I once was inclined
> To strip down
> And grease up
> And bliss out my mind.
> I was a solar collector,
> A barefoot boy with his reflector,
> A Coppertone Pro-Am,
> George Hamilton was my protector.
> I came to
> Tan, tan, tan, tan.
> Tan, tan, tan, tan.
> Tan, tan, tan, tan.

PLANTS (*sing*):
> Oh, what risks they ran,
> Those boys who dared to tan,
> Those brown boys we adored,
> Here's to you, Jack Lord.

ALL (*sing*):
> Got to, got to, got to tan, tan, tan, tan.

At this point, ZONKER *has a flashback to the glory days of his tanning career. He is in the finals of the George Hamilton Pro-Am Cocoa Butter Open. As he throws out his chest,* DAN *and his color commentator,* SKIP, *enter stage right.*

DAN: And with the final heat almost over, Harris is heading into the stretch! It's Zonker Harris all the way!

SKIP: And what a glow he's got, Dan. The talented youngster out of Marin County seems to have developed his kind of tan. Talk about technique! Look at the thrust of his chest! Harris is really pouring it on!

DAN: He is indeed, Skip. You know, a lot of people thought Harris could only make it in the sun sprints—

SKIP: That's right.

DAN: —But he's shown here today that he's up there with the big boys now.

SKIP: Dan, as you know, Harris has been plagued in the past by unevenness and peeling, but today he seems to have achieved full color balance with a flashy, tropical tan—the kind of primitive, precancerous glow so favored by the young hotshots on the circuit these days.

DAN: And there he goes into his final curl; five seconds left, four, three, two, one! He's done it! Zonker Harris has won the George Hamilton Pro-Am Cocoa Butter Open! Let's see if we can get a word with the new champ. Zonker? Zonker?

SKIP: What a competitor, Dan.

DAN: Right you are, Skip. The man definitely came to tan. Zonker, anything you'd like to say to aspiring young tannists watching today?

ZONKER: Absolutely. (*Sings.*)
You got to, got to, got to
Tan, tan, tan, tan.

SCENE 3

Los Angeles County Courtroom. Present. Day. We cut to DUKE*'s trial. Under the stern gaze of the presiding* JUDGE, DUKE *is sitting in the witness chair facing the jury. Off to one side,* HONEY *waits to be called as a character witness.*

JUDGE: If only for the jurors' entertainment, let's run your story by them one more time, shall we? If I understand you correctly, you are asking this Court to believe you purchased ten kilograms of cocaine at the direction of the State Department?

DUKE: That is correct.

The JUDGE *laughs.*

HONEY: That *is* a little farfetched, sir.

DUKE: Look, I haven't got the time or the patience for any more of this. I'm a former United States Ambassador to China, for God's sake. If you don't believe my story, call George Shultz at State and he'll confirm that—

JUDGE: As the District Attorney has already indicated, Mr. Duke, Secretary Shultz has sworn in an affidavit that he has never heard of any plan to stock our diplomatic missions with recreational drugs.

DUKE: And you believed him? Jesus Christ! Those guys are *paid* to lie! What the hell happened to equal justice in this country? Missile-mongers like Shultz are walking around free as birds, while a public servant of my stature is chained to a witness stand and worked over by some fat political appointee and a handpicked collection of surly ethnics, drooling senior citizens, laid-off postal clerks, and former mental patients. My God! You call this a jury of my peers? We are talking human garbage here!

JUDGE (*looking at his watch*): Let me know when you've finished playing to the jury's sympathies.

DUKE (*to the jury*): I'm innocent, goddammit!

JUDGE: The jury will bear in mind, of course, that our prisons are full of so-called innocent men.

DUKE: Prison? Who said anything about prison?

HONEY: Psst, sir. I think it's time to change your strategy.

DUKE: Shut up, Honey. I can handle this. (*To* JUDGE): Listen, you swinehead.

JUDGE (*writing*): Before we go on, let me just add a contempt citation to the charges—

The situation clearly getting out of hand, DUKE *sees that, indeed, it is time for a change in strategy.*

DUKE: Okay. Okay. You win. Happy? You want to know why I did it? Okay, I'll tell you why. I did it for the money.

JUDGE: Please imagine the Court's surprise.

DUKE: But you want to know why I needed the money? What I said before . . . about doing it on orders from Shultz . . . that wasn't true.

HONEY: Sir! That's perjury!

DUKE: He *knows* what it is, Honey.

JUDGE: Come to the point, Mr. Duke.

DUKE: As I said . . . I needed the money. . . . In fact, I needed it desperately. The picture I'm going to paint for you may not be a pretty one, but it is a story of truth and compassion, so I want to dedicate it to every one of you in the jury.

JUDGE: The jury will disregard the defendant's dedication.

HONEY: This better be good, sir.

JUDGE (*tapping his watch*): Mr. Duke?

DUKE (*sings*):
Thanks, Your Honor,
I'll try to keep it short.

I know I haven't told it straight 'til now, but . . .
Please the Court,
I'm just a man
Who's been misunderstood.
Yeah, I'm guilty of carin',
Guilty of sharin',
Too much for my own good.
When I was in China,
I was like a lonely marine.
I talked to lots of pretty little local girls,
And whores in between.
And though I up and left
As soon as I could,
Those women were bearin'
The fruit of my carin'
Too much for my own good.
I sent them traveler's checks,
But they were never enough.
With five of 'em sick and twelve in school,
Well, those youngsters had it rough.
I couldn't rest
'Til they had the best
In stereos and jeans,
You know, good American stuff.
My friends, if you could see their faces
In that far-off hell,
I gotta picture here of my youngest . . . Oh, damn, I . . .
Musta left it in my cell.
I know I think of others
More than I should.
Yeah, I'm guilty of carin',
Guilty of sharin',
Too much for my own good.
Yeah, I'm guilty of carin',
Guilty of sharin',
Too much for my own good.

HONEY: Sir? Were you really dating around in Peking?

SCENE 4

Walden Commune. Day. MIKE *is dialing the phone while he flips through a plastic index card file.* MARK *is sitting on the sofa. To the right of the living room set, we see another telephone set up on a small table. As it begins to ring,* J.J. *enters stage left at a dead run.*

J.J. (*answers phone out of breath*): Hello?

MIKE (*reading from a card*): "Hi, J.J., it's me, Mike. Just checking to see if you're still coming up for the big Dartmouth game this . . ." Damn!

J.J.: What?

MIKE *frantically starts flipping through his files again.*

J.J.: What Dartmouth game?

MIKE (*buying time*): Well, no, not the Dartmouth game, obviously. . . . I mean, that was last fall, wasn't it? During the football season . . .

J.J.: I guess so. Listen, Mike, I can't talk. I'm trying to make the 3:05.

MIKE (*locating the right card*): "J.J.? Hi, it's me, Mike. I was just calling to see what train you'd be on . . ."

J.J.: I just told you, the 3:05. Mike, you're not still using those dumb cards, are you?

MIKE *looks up from his card.*

MIKE: Uh . . . no. Well, yes.

J.J.: Michael. You promised me that you'd stop.

MIKE: I know, I know, I know. It's just I'm . . . I'm a little on edge today. You know, with graduation and everything. I mean, everyone's going to be here. My brother's flying in, Joanie's coming up—

J.J.: Whoa. Wait a minute. You asked my mother?

MIKE: Well, of course, J.J. I couldn't not ask her.

MARK *and* ZONKER *enter with* JOANIE. JOANIE *is carrying a baby.*

MIKE: Joanie spent almost three years here living with us.

J.J.: Oh, Michael, how could you?

ZONKER: Hey, Mike. Look who we found!

JOANIE: Ta da!

MARK: The return of the den mother, disguised as a normal person.

MIKE: Joanie!

J.J.: Oh, God. I can't believe you asked her.

MIKE: Uh, J.J. . . . I can't . . .

JOANIE: J.J.? Oh, is she coming, too?

MIKE: Uh . . . yes. Hey, you brought the baby!

MARK: Cute little sucker, isn't he?

J.J.: The baby? Great. That's just great. Some weekend, Mike.

JOANIE: Jeffrey, say hello to Michael.

J.J.: Look, I gotta go. Thanks a lot, Mike. I really needed this. Bye.

J.J. *slams down the receiver and exits.*

MIKE: What? Uh . . . right. I'll give them your love. I know she's looking forward to seeing you, too. See you soon. Bye.

He hangs up.

JOANIE: J.J. really said she's looking forward to seeing me?

MIKE *holds out his arms to the baby.*

MIKE: So this is Jeffrey.

ZONKER: Pretty nice piece of work, huh?

MIKE: Absolutely. He's beautiful, Joanie.

JOANIE: Thank you, Michael.

MARK: Actually, you're not looking too shabby yourself, counselor. What happened to the stringy hair and granny dresses?

JOANIE *does a little curtsy.*

JOANIE: Enough gabardine for you? This is what happens when you get run over by a major law firm.

ZONKER: God. How frightening. They actually make you wear uniforms?

BOOPSIE *enters from her bedroom.*

BOOPSIE: Has anyone seen my . . . (*Spotting* JOANIE): Joanie!

JOANIE: Hello, Boopsie, dear.

BOOPSIE: You brought the baby! Oh, I want one.

ZONKER: You do?

MARK: So much for your new career.

JOANIE: What career?

MARK: Well, maybe "career" is too strong a word.

MIKE: Cheerleading. B.D. got drafted by Dallas, so Boopsie's trying out for the Cowgirls.

JOANIE: The Cowgirls. Imagine that.

BOOPSIE: It's only temporary. Cheerleading's just a stepping-stone to jobs as a serious film actress.

MARK: The woman's drunk with ambition.

ZONKER: And what happens to your baby while you're out prancing around in your underwear all day?

BOOPSIE: Well, after I get established, I'll take the baby to the stadium with me. I'll just have it put in my contract. Everything's possible if you want it bad enough. I learned that from Joanie.

JOANIE: You did?

BOOPSIE: You taught me that a woman doesn't have to settle, that she can go for it, that she can have a demanding career and outside interests and friends and hobbies and a fulfilling marriage with lots of sex and mutual respect and children all at the same time.

JOANIE: I said that?

MARK: I'm afraid so, counselor.

MIKE: You were young. You oversold.

BOOPSIE (*sings*):
    You smiled at me,
    You said, "Load up your plate,
    Dare to be great,
    Go for the gold, it's worth the wait."
    Well, you made me see,
    I should dress for success,
    Get lots of rest,
    Budget my time and look my best,
    Then I can have it all,
    Can have it all,
    Can have it all.
    So I . . .

MEN (*sing*):
    Took your advice.

BOOPSIE (*sings*):
    Told my guy . . .

MEN (*sing*):
    This part is nice.

BOOPSIE (*sings*):
    He should swallow his pride,
    Stay by my side,
    Stick with his chick for the ride.
    Then he . . .

MEN (*sing*):
    This part is sad.

BOOPSIE (*sings*):
    He saw red.

MEN (*sing*):
    That boy was mad.

BOOPSIE (*sings*):
    But I had to break through,
    Make my debut,
    Gear up to cheer for you-know-who.
    Now I . . .

MEN (*sing*):
　　She'll shout it loud.

BOOPSIE (*sings*):
　　Can have it all.

MEN (*sing*):
　　She'll draw a crowd.

BOOPSIE (*sings*):
　　Can have it all.

MEN (*sing, to* JOANIE):
　　You must be proud.

BOOPSIE (*sings*):
　　Can have it all.
　　I know I can handle
　　Both ends of the candle,
　　I ain't gonna fake it,
　　No, no, no,
　　I'm achin' to make it,
　　I can have it all.
　　Gonna have it all, kids and career.
　　Gonna have it by this time next year.
　　Doncha know that my dreams just won't quit.
　　And you know that I'm gonna go get it,
　　Gonna go get it now,
　　Gonna go get it,
　　Gonna go get it,
　　Doncha know I'm gonna go,
　　Gonna go get it,
　　Gonna go get it,
　　Gonna go get it now.
　　Yeah, I . . .

MEN (*sing*):
　　It's understood . . .

BOOPSIE (*sings*):
　　Can have it all.

MEN (*sing*):
　　She'll have it good.

BOOPSIE (*sings*):
  Can have it all.

MEN (*sing, to* JOANIE):
  You said she could.

BOOPSIE (*sings*):
  Can have it all.
  I can have it.
  I can have it.
  I can have it all.

As BOOPSIE *finishes singing,* B.D. *enters from his bedroom.*

JOANIE: I'm . . . I'm speechless.

B.D.: Now, that's a switch.

JOANIE: B.D.!

B.D.: How's it goin', Caucus?

JOANIE: It's goin' great, dear. I hear you're following Boopsie to Dallas.

B.D.: You heard I'm what?

BOOPSIE: Oh, not for a couple weeks yet, Joanie. We're going down to Memphis first.

JOANIE: Memphis? What's in Memphis?

B.D.: You don't want to know. Come on, Boopsie, we're gonna be late.

BOOPSIE: We're taking a four-day, three-night Elvis tour.

MIKE: Elvis tour?

B.D.: Four days? Hold it. It's going to take us four whole days just to genuflect at Elvis' grave?

BOOPSIE: Oh, there's a lot more to do than just that, B.D., if you really want to do Elvis.

JOANIE: People "do" Elvis?

BOOPSIE: In fact, if you included the mansion at Graceland, his gravesite, the studios he recorded in, and all his girlfriends' homes, you'd need at least ten days.

B.D.: That's ridiculous. Hell, France only takes a week.

BOOPSIE: B.D., it's only the most popular pilgrimage package tour in America. In fact, over three million of the King's fans—

B.D.: Boopsie, enough! Come on, we don't want to keep the folks waiting.

BOOPSIE: See you later, Joanie.

BOOPSIE *kisses the baby and gets up.*

JOANIE: Bye, dear.

BOOPSIE: B.D. and I are meeting my parents for lunch.

B.D.: Should be fun. They still think Boopsie's applying for a Fulbright.

B.D. *and* BOOPSIE *exit.*

JOANIE: Oh, you guys, come sit down. I want to hear all your plans.

ZONKER: Well, if you mean career plans, I'm still a little undecided. But that's normal for someone of my age and build. The important thing is I have a place to live. We've decided to stay on here at Walden.

MIKE: Now, wait a minute, Zonker. That's not exactly certain, either.

ZONKER: Sure it is. I'm going by Mrs. Kirby's tomorrow to renew the lease.

MIKE: Zonker, it's not that simple.

MARK: Yeah, who knows? One of us might decide to get married.

MIKE (*angrily*): Mark!

ZONKER *looks up at* MARK *with surprise.*

ZONKER: Mark?

MARK: No, Mike.

MIKE: Mark!

JOANIE: Mike?

ZONKER: Mike. Right. (*To* JOANIE): They like to do this to me. It's because I'm from California, where anything is possible.

JOANIE (*slowly*): Michael? Are you planning to marry my daughter?

MIKE: Thanks a lot, Mark.

ZONKER (*covering ears and humming*): I'm not falling for this, guys.

JOANIE: Have you and J.J. discussed this yet?

MIKE: No, no, we haven't. I was planning on asking her tomorrow.

JOANIE *hands the baby to* ZONKER *and gets up to hug* MIKE.

ZONKER (*to* MARK): Okay, let me get this straight. Mike is actually considering marriage in real life?

MARK: Yup.

ZONKER: And you condone it?

MARK: No. I'm the loyal opposition. But if she moves in here, it's one more person to share the rent.

ZONKER's *face brightens. He hands* JEFFREY *to* MARK *and then crosses over to* MIKE.

ZONKER: May I be the very first to congratulate both you and your lovely fiancée?

MIKE: Yes, you may. But you'll have to wait until I have one.

ZONKER: I'm sure it'll work out. We'll so look forward to welcoming J.J. here just as we did her mother before her. You can have her old room.

JOANIE: It does have a nice kind of symmetry to it.

ZONKER: Boy, this plan is really beginning to come together. (ZONKER *heads for the door.*) I gotta go turn the compost heap. See you at dinner. (ZONKER *exits.*)

MIKE (*running after him*): Zonker! Zonker!

MARK (*to* MIKE): There's no turning back now. Zonker's involved.

JOANIE: He's not the only one. I didn't expect this kind of cross-pollination quite so soon. (*She looks at* JEFFREY *squirming in her lap.*) Be honest, guys. Do I look like I'm ready to become a grandmother?

MIKE and MARK: Sure. No problem there. Uh-huh.

SCENE 5

Los Angeles County Courtroom. We open on DUKE *and* HONEY *conferring in the back of the courtoom.*

DUKE: I gotta hand it to you, Honey, that was some testimony. I'm talking state-of-the-art bullshit. Where'd you learn to give such great character witness?

HONEY: Well, sir, during the last purge I was chief witness for Madam Mao and the Gang of Four.

DUKE: Gang of Four? No kidding. You know, Honey, maybe I've underestimated you all these years. If I get through this, how'd you like to be my Gal Friday?

HONEY: At the risk of being forward, sir, I'm free the whole week.

The JUDGE *enters and bangs his gavel.*

JUDGE: The court will please come to order. The jury has found the defendant . . . (*He unfolds a piece of paper.*) . . . guilty as charged.

DUKE: Guilty? This is an outrage! (*Turning on the jury*): I'll get you. I'll track down every last one of you if it takes the rest of my life!

JUDGE: The defendant will approach the bench for sentencing. Mr. Duke, in light of the compelling testimony of your former translator—

DUKE: Lies! All of it!

JUDGE: I would hope not, Mr. Duke. Indeed, Miss Huan's assurances as to your tireless devotion to public service and your general excellence of character prompts this Court to place you on probation with the provision that as penance, you are to forthwith establish and direct a drug rehabilitation center for a period of no less than five years. It is the Court's profound hope that in so doing, you will spare a future generation of miscreants the chronic degradation and self-abuse from which you yourself have suffered so deeply. Court adjourned.

The JUDGE *bangs his gavel and retires.*

DUKE: Drug rehabilitation center? (*He laughs, maniacally.*) I love it! Honey! Saddle up! We ride again!

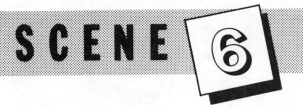

SCENE 6

The White House scrim.

AIDE: Mr. President? Secretary Clark here to see you, sir.

REAGAN: Bill, come in. I hear your first meetings with the environmental groups went very well.

CLARK: Well, sir, I was ready for them. I spent a whole week at home working with my wildlife flash cards. I did have some problems with the acid rain question, though, and I'd like to know how you want me to handle it. We've been getting a lot of heat from Canada lately; in fact, the Canadians are beginning to threaten economic sanctions against us.

REAGAN: Gosh, that's terrible. Could we invade?

CLARK: I'll check to see if there are any American lives that need protecting.

SCENE 7

Walden Commune. As we open, MARK *is on the phone while* MIKE *sits in his swivel chair working on his schedule.*

MARK (*into phone*): Good of you to confirm, Roland. I'll be looking for your limo out at the radio station sometime after five.

J.J. enters through the front door. She is carrying a knapsack.

J.J.: Hi ya, Slim. Hey, Mark.

MARK *waves to her.*

MARK: See you soon. Bye-bye.

MIKE: J.J.! What are you doing here?

J.J.: You invited me, remember?

MIKE: But you're . . . (*Checks watch.*) You're eleven minutes early.

J.J.: Am I going to have to wait eleven minutes for a hug?

MIKE: No . . . no, of course not.

He goes over and hugs her. MARK *heads for the door.*

MARK: Well, I better be tooling along, kids. Tune me in at 5:30 if you've got absolutely nothing better to do.

MIKE *and* J.J. *are locked in an embrace.*

MARK: Fat chance.

MARK *exits.*

MIKE: Boy, it's good to see you. You look great.

MIKE *helps* J.J. *off with her coat.*

J.J.: You're lookin' pretty slick yourself, kid. Is she around?

MIKE: Joanie? Uh . . . no, she's out shopping.

J.J.: Look, I gotta be honest with you, Mike. I'm here because you're graduating. But if she gets on my case, I'm just splitting.

MIKE: Splitting? Hey, no, you don't want to do that. We got big plans today.

J.J.: We do?

MIKE: You better believe it. Here, take a look at this.

MIKE *picks up his schedule, snaps out a carbon copy, and hands it to her.*

J.J.: What is it?

MIKE: Our weekend schedule. That's your copy. You can keep it.

J.J.: Oh. Thanks. Where's it start?

MIKE: Right here where it says "4:15, J.J. arrives at house." Of course, we'll have to adjust that now, won't we? Let me get you a pencil.

J.J. (*reading*): "4:15, J.J. arrives at house; 4:20–4:25, Mike gets dinner in the oven while J.J. unwinds with a fast glass of wine . . ."

MIKE: Well, it doesn't have to be wine. This thing's pretty flexible. Anyway, at 4:30 sharp, after you finish unwinding, we go over to the quad for the big senior class softball game, which should be over by 6:10. Then from 6:15 to 6:45, I finish up dinner while you get to know my friends a little better so they won't think of you as a mere appendage of me but actually accept you as a person in your own right. Okay. Now, that's followed at 7:00 by—

J.J.: Michael, wait a minute. This is a little overwhelming. What if we feel like just doing nothing, you know, just sitting out on the porch, not saying a word?

MIKE: 11:15 to 11:45. I'm way ahead of you.

J.J.: Michael, have you planned out your whole life this way?

MIKE: My whole life? Don't be silly. (*A beat.*) Some of it.

J.J.: Like what?

MIKE: Um . . . well, you know about business school, of course. As for the rest . . . well, you know . . . nothing definite. It depends.

J.J.: Yeah, same with me. It depends.

BOTH (*sing*):
I've been thinking . . . what?

J.J. (*sings*):
No, please, please, go ahead, you were saying . . .

MIKE (*sings*):
I was talking off the top of my head.
I just thought . . .

J.J. (*sings*):
You just thought . . .

MIKE (*sings*):
That I might move on.

J.J. (*sings*):
Really.

MIKE (*sings*):
Find some sort of place
Of my own whereupon
I was thinking . . .

J.J. (*sings*):
You were thinking . . .

MIKE (*sings*):
Well, I guess that I was hoping . . .

J.J. (*sings*):
Hoping what?

MIKE (*sings*):
No. It's dumb.
We'll be too busy coping,
There's all sorts of problems for us to weather,
But sometime soon we should try
To get together,
If it's okay with you.

J.J.: "Get together"?

MIKE (*sings*):
Spend a few days with you.

BOTH (*sing*):
   Yeah, sometime soon we should try to get together.

MIKE: So, how about you?

J.J.: Well . . . (*sings*):
   I found a studio apartment
   Over by the art school,
   Haven't signed the lease yet . . .

MIKE (*sings*):
   Hey, that's cool,
   I can understand that
   You need to be a . . .

J.J. (*sings*):
   A person in my own right.

MIKE (*sings*):
   I completely agree.
   You should have your own friends . . .

J.J. (*sings*):
   I'm bound to make a few . . .

MIKE (*sings*):
   We shouldn't be like bookends,
   Don't you think that's true?

J.J. (*sings*):
   I should go it alone,
   If that's okay with you,
   But sometime soon we should try
   To get together . . .

MIKE (*sings*):
   Like to see you some more . . .

J.J. (*sings*):
   Get together . . .

MIKE (*sings*):
   I could sleep on the floor.

BOTH (*sing*):
   Yeah, sometime soon we should try to get together.

Oh, I've known since I found you,
I want to be around you,
But not be in your way,
We'll take it day by day.
Oh, I'll always be there for you,
It turns out I adore you,
So if I'm passing by,
I might give you a try.

J.J. (*sings*):
And sometime soon we should try to get together . . .

MIKE (*sings*):
Sometime soon we should try to get together.

BOTH (*sing*):
Oooo, try to get together.

As song ends, J.J. *crosses to sofa and sits.* JOANIE *enters with bag of groceries.*

MIKE: Joanie! (*To* J.J.): Look who's here.

J.J. *looks at her mother but says nothing.*

MIKE: It's your mother.

JOANIE: Hello, J.J.

J.J.: Hello, Mother.

JOANIE: Is Jeffrey still sleeping?

MIKE: He's out cold. Here, let me give you a hand with that.

He takes the bag from JOANIE.

MIKE: Well, Joanie, as you can see, J.J.'s a little early, and we seem to have some discretionary time on our hands here, so why don't we all just sit down and . . .

JOANIE: Oh, hey, no, Mike. I'm sure you and J.J. would like to be alone.

MIKE: Don't be silly. J.J. and I have the whole rest of the weekend to-gether. It's the perfect time for you two to just shoot the breeze and get caught up.

He finally manages to get JOANIE *to sit on the arm of the couch. He then sits down between them.*

MIKE: Okay. Here we go. J.J.?

J.J. *sighs deeply.*

J.J.: So how's Dick?

MIKE: Rick. Your stepfather's name is Rick.

J.J.: Rick. Right.

JOANIE: He's fine, thanks. Everything okay at school?

J.J.: Suddenly she cares.

MIKE: Great answer.

JOANIE: J.J., has this terrible anger become permanent?

J.J.: You were hoping it was just a stage?

JOANIE: I didn't say that.

MIKE: She didn't say that, J.J.

J.J.: Well, it's always a stage with you, isn't it, Mother? Each conflict is just one more way station on the road to personhood.

JOANIE: Is that such a bad place to end up?

J.J.: I wouldn't know, Mom. It's your fantasy.

J.J. *starts to get up, but* MIKE *restrains her.*

MIKE: Hey, hey, hey. Okay, now obviously, there's a certain amount of tension in the room right now. You guys have to work this out. Now, I'd be willing to open up a slot here—

J.J.: Michael—

MIKE: No, no, I insist. You guys need some time to yourselves. And I'm talking quantity time here, not just quality time. Now, I had set aside 25 minutes to get drunk before the concert tonight—

JOANIE: Michael. No.

MIKE: Joanie, this can't go on like this. It's obvious that J.J. still doesn't really understand why you left.

JOANIE: Michael, she doesn't want to understand. We've been over it a million times and—

J.J.: Understand? What's to understand? Mother just couldn't handle all the bowling and barbecues and car pools, so she just split. It's one of those poignant feminist folk tales of the '70s.

JOANIE: That's it, J.J. If you think I'm just going to stand here and listen to you dismiss ten years of my life, you're crazy. What we did was not unimportant.

J.J.: We? Who's we? The Movement? What did the Movement ever do for me? Do you know how boring all that is, Mother? Liberation? The Cause? It's like when Grandma talks about the Depression.

JOANIE: Well, there you have it, Michael. The voice of the new wave. Injustice is boring.

MIKE: She didn't say that, Joanie. . . .

JOANIE: My God. Can your world really be that narrow? Can you really believe the choices were that simple?

J.J.: I am woman, hear me hyperventilate!

JOANIE: Goddammit, Joan, you weren't the only one who was hurt!

MIKE: That's right. I think Sylvia Plath put it best . . .

J.J.: No, but somebody left and somebody was left behind. Somebody moved into a commune and raised other people's children, and someone raised herself on her own. It doesn't interest me that you managed to justify it as political statement, Mother. It doesn't interest me that you chose to spend eight years sitting around with bitter, unhappy women discussing your pain instead of being with me. How was I supposed to identify with all that? I just wanted a mother.

J.J. runs out the front door.

MIKE: J.J., wait a minute.

JOANIE: So much for quality time.

JOANIE exits into the bedroom, leaving MIKE alone. MIKE is totally undone by the storm he has created. He looks at his watch.

MIKE: Oh, God.

MIKE runs out after J.J.

SCENE 8

WABY radio station. MARK *and* ROLAND *are seated behind a console desk.*

MIKE, ZONKER, BOOPSIE (*sing, voice-over*):
Marvelous Mark. Profiles on parade!

MARK: And we're back. In case you've just joined us, this is Marvelous Mark talking with top television correspondent Roland Burton Hedley, Jr. Okay, Roland, I'm going to take a page from your own book and go right to the tough questions.

ROLAND: Turning the tables, eh? Hey, fair enough. Shoot.

MARK: Okay. What's the inside story on your Nicaraguan makeup man?

ROLAND: Domingo? Legitimate question, Mark. Domingo was first assigned to me just before the fall of Managua. He also handled wardrobe for the U.N. mediators, and I think he was doing hair for the Sandinistas. I recall one day he was almost blown away at a checkpoint when the National Guard mistook his big 1200-watt hairblower for a concealed Uzi. Of course, those sorts of risks come with the business. As I was telling Fred Cronkite the other night—

MARK: Fred Cronkite? Who's that?

ROLAND: Well, you may know him as Walter Cronkite. His good friends call him Fred. At least, that's what I've heard. Anyway, as I was telling him and "Mad Jack" Chancellor last night, we're paid to look death in the teeth. Sure, being a foreign correspondent means you're going to have your moments of truth, your baptisms of fire, your bad room service. But you can't dwell on it. When you're on a mission, you can't afford to lose your concentration or get attached to anything—including your own life.

MARK: Well, it seems like you're always in some kind of hot water, Roland. I'm reminded of the time you asked Yasser Arafat why he always wears exactly three days' growth of beard.

ROLAND: That's right, Mark, Chairman Arafat—or "Ol' Raghead," as we used to call him—revealed to me exclusively that his contract with the PLO requires him to look "homeless" and "down on his luck" at all times. ABC Wide World of News was first with that story, by the way.

MARK: As it has been with so many others just like it. Okay, coming up on fifteen minutes after the hour, we'll be back after these brief commercial messages.

MARK *flips a switch on the console.*

MIKE, ZONKER, BOOPSIE (*sing, voice-over*):
Marvelous Mark. Profiles on parade.

ROLAND *leans back in his chair.*

ROLAND: Very impressive interview, Mark. Most penetrating. You have a great career in broadcast journalism ahead of you, son.

MARK: Well, not unless one of the 185 stations I sent my tape to has a change of heart.

ROLAND: What?

MARK: The jobs just aren't out there. Especially for the kind of show I do.

ROLAND: But what about this station? Surely you're the biggest draw they've ever had.

MARK: They're not hiring either.

ROLAND: You're selling yourself short, son. Why don't you make an appeal on the air? Make a pitch. What have you got to lose?

MARK: Well, now that you mention it, nothing.

ROLAND: Then go for it. Never underestimate the power of an aroused audience.

MARK *nods and slams a cassette into a playback machine.*

ANNOUNCER (*voice-over*): So if you can't find a job, get the full story on food stamps. Food stamps. Because this is America, not Bangladesh.

MARK: And we are back, campers. But not for long. Unless you speak out, a great voice is about to be stilled.

ROLAND: This is ABC News correspondent Roland Burton Hedley, Jr., and if you believe, as I do, that Marvelous Mark is a major talent waiting to explode on the media scene, then you'll let the management of this station hear about it. Give us a call at . . .

MARK: Seven eight seven, forty-three eleven.

ROLAND: That's seven eight seven, forty-three eleven. Call now.

MARK (*raps*):
   Think they'll do it?

ROLAND (*raps*):
   If you give it a goose.

MARK (*raps*):
   You mean, fire 'em up?

ROLAND (*raps*):
   Sure, turn on the juice.

MARK (*raps*):
   Okay, campers, gotta say yes.
   Tell me in twenty-five words or less,
   Why Marvelous Mark is the man of the hour,
   Got the glory, got the power.
   You've saved the whales, now save the Man,
   Don't let Mark be a flash in the pan,
   No! Give us a call for the talent that shines,
   Give us the word, say the lines . . .
   Say "I want Mark,
   Love his bark.
   He's got my support,
   I'll make it short,
   Keep Mark at the fort."
   He's got moves.
   The guy's pure sex.
   But a man's got needs,
   Like weekly salary checks.

ROLAND (*raps*):
  He's a pistol
  And he's thorough,
  He could be the next Ed Murrow.
  He's a heavy,
  Plain to see,
  He might even be the next me.

MARK (*raps*):
  Gotta save his silky, rich baritone,
  The rants and the chants on the call-in phone,
  His political savvy, his incredible wit,
  So pick up the phone and throw a fit.
  Call in campers, today.
  What you all got to say?

FIRST CALLER (*raps*):
  I think Marvelous Mark
  Is a ten!

MARK (*raps*):
  Say again?

FIRST CALLER (*raps*):
  He's a ten!

MARK (*raps*):
  Once again?

FIRST CALLER (*raps*):
  He's a ten!

MARK (*raps*):
  That's it, campers, oh my,
  I'm turnin' up the volume high.

SECOND CALLER (*raps*):
  I say . . .

MARK (*raps*):
  Say what?

SECOND CALLER (*raps*):
  That Marvelous Mark
  Is a marvelous . . .

MARK (*raps*):
 Marvelous?

SECOND CALLER (*raps*):
 Guy!

MARK (*raps*):
 Let's lay a handle on him.
 Who wants to take the lead?

THIRD CALLER (*raps*):
 He's a legend.

FOURTH CALLER (*raps*):
 A god.

FIFTH CALLER (*raps*):
 A state of mind.

SIXTH CALLER (*raps*):
 A schemer.

SEVENTH CALLER (*raps*):
 A dreamer.

ALL (*rap*):
 For all mankind!

MARK (*raps*):
 Say I want Mark.

ALL (*rap*):
 Want Mark.

MARK (*raps*):
 The guy's pure sex.

ALL (*rap*):
 Pure sex.

MARK (*raps*):
 But a man's got needs.

ALL (*rap*):
 Got needs.

MARK (*raps*):
 Like weekly salary checks.

ALL (*rap*):
 Weekly salary checks.

FIRST CALLER (*raps*):
 Save our baby boom boogie boy.

SECOND CALLER (*raps*):
 Put that brother in your employ.

THIRD CALLER (*raps*):
 Keep him from easin' on down the pike.

FOURTH CALLER (*raps*):
 Catch him, patch him . . .

SIXTH CALLER (*raps*):
 And attach him to his mike.

SEVENTH CALLER (*raps*):
 He's in danger.

ALL (*rap*):
 We don't care
 For some stranger on the air!

MARK (*raps*):
 Say I want Mark.

ALL (*rap*):
 Want Mark.

MARK (*raps*):
 The guy's pure sex.

ALL (*rap*):
 Pure sex.

MARK (*raps*):
 But a man's got needs.

ALL (*rap*):
 Got needs.

MARK (*raps*):
 Like weekly salary checks.

ALL (*rap*):
 Weekly salary checks.

MARK (*raps*):
Well, you gotta believe we're on a roll,
It's perkin' and it's workin'
And it's out of control.
Campers don't be afraid
To join the Mark Crusade.

FOURTH CALLER (*raps*):
I feel . . .

MARK (*raps*):
Feel what?

FOURTH CALLER (*raps*):
That Marvelous Mark
Should be handsomely . . .

MARK (*raps*):
Handsomely?

FOURTH CALLER (*raps*):
Paid!

MARK *stands up and starts to break dance.*

MARK (*raps*):
This is such a thrill it sends a chill right through my spine,
I feel from your direction a connection of affection,
Say it a little louder,
Make me a little prouder,
FM fans, oh yeah,
They tend to be ecstatic,
And more idiosyncratic
Than your video fanatic,
I'm so wired and admired I'm inspired to be hired,
Well, I feel I'm a steal,
I'm a real baby boom boogie catch,
It's such a bitchin' itchin' that you're helping me to scratch.
Gotta go for global glory, gotta get on down and share
The funky hunky-dory of my story on the air.
Now one more time,
A righteous rhyme,
Convey to me and lay on me

A sign of excitation
From the clients of this station,
With a fine appreciation
Of my baby boom bark.
Say, Save our Mark.
That's the way, you got to Save our Mark.
Save the day, people. Save our Mark. Uh, huh.
Now this.

SCENE 9

Walden Commune. Later that day. As we open, MIKE *is in the kitchen preparing dinner. Out in the living room,* ZONKER *is trying to build a beer can pyramid on top of the television.* JOANIE *is at the dinner table, discreetly nursing her baby, while beside her on the floor,* BOOPSIE *is doing exercises.*

B.D. *enters from his bedroom and walks into the kitchen.*

B.D.: What's the story with dinner, Mike? Another ten minutes and I'm ordering a pizza.

MIKE: Almost finished.

BOOPSIE (*puffing*): 196 . . . 197 . . . 198 . . . 199 . . . 1 . . . 200.

B.D. *looks over at* BOOPSIE *and shakes his head.*

B.D.: Hey, Boopsie. Boopsie!

BOOPSIE: What?

B.D.: Give it a rest, will ya? You look like an ad for a Swiss army knife.

BOOPSIE: In a sec. I gotta finish my abdominals.

B.D.: Come on, Boopsie, we're about to have dinner here, and you're sweating all over the carpet.

BOOPSIE: B.D., the workout isn't effective if you skip any of the exercises.

JOANIE: What sort of program are you on, dear?

BOOPSIE: Jane Fonda's. I've been doing it for a while, and you wouldn't believe the results you get. It firms you up *and* develops your political sensitivity at the same time.

B.D.: What a crock.

BOOPSIE: It is not, B.D. There's a proven connection between activism and being in shape.

JOANIE: What are you active in, dear?

BOOPSIE: Well, mostly the Freeze. Actually, I've been involved ever since Reagan got elected. That guy just scares me to death.

JOANIE: You and a lot of other women, Boopsie. That's why he's faced with such a large gender gap.

B.D. *looks up from his magazine.*

B.D.: A large *what*?

JOANIE: Gender gap.

B.D.: That's disgusting.

JOANIE: B.D., gender gap just means—

B.D. *gets up.*

B.D.: I don't want to know what it means. (B.D. *goes into the kitchen.*) Okay, Mike, when the hell's dinner? Happy hour just peaked.

MIKE: Two more minutes. Here, go to work on this.

MIKE *hands* B.D. *a beer.* B.D. *wheels around and returns to the living room.*

B.D.: You want to know what your problem is, Caucus? You always gotta provoke people, you know? You never let up, you— (*For the first time, he notices that* JOANIE *is breast-feeding the baby.*) Oh, Jesus, you're doing it again. (*To* BOOPSIE): See? She's doing it again.

ZONKER: Doing what? What's Joanie doing?

JOANIE: I'm just nursing Jeffrey, Zonker.

ZONKER: Oh. I'm building a beer can pyramid.

B.D. (*to* BOOPSIE): Can you believe this? The woman just isn't happy if she isn't causing a scene.

MARK *enters through the front door.*

MARK (*raps*): Gotta save his silky rich baritone. The rants and the chants on the call-in phone. His political savvy, his incredible wit . . . so pick up the phone and throw a fit! Friends! I have just scaled the heights of Parnassus.

B.D.: This is why the ERA never passed, you know. Because the women who supported it were always grossing everyone out.

MARK: Put another way, I have just seen God.

JOANIE: B.D., if I'd known it was going to upset you so, I'd have just gone out into the garage.

MARK: How'd my last show go, you ask? Well, it was an event. Three hundred and fourteen callers, all demanding that I be put on salary.

ZONKER: You know, this is actually a lot trickier than it looks.

MARK: How do I feel? In a word, gratified. Touched. Moved, if you will.

ZONKER: Oh, hi, Mark. How'd your last show go?

MIKE *sticks his head out of the kitchen door.*

MIKE: Soup's on. Everyone to the table.

MARK: You'll be sorry. You all will. Because when I reach the top, I'm having you all put to death.

J.J. *enters from bedroom.*

J.J.: Hi, everyone.

MIKE (*calling* J.J. *to one side*): J.J.?

J.J.: Hey, chef, need any help?

MIKE: No, I've got it all under control. Are you sure you're going to be okay here?

J.J.: I told you, Mike, I won't lose it again. Don't worry. What are we having?

MIKE: You'll see. You just go sit down and—

J.J. (*spotting the salad*): Mike! Is that seaweed? It is. You made me a seaweed salad!

MIKE: Yeah. Fresh kelp, lettuce, and sprouts. The lettuce was organically grown. I even left the dirt on.

J.J. (*looking at the salad*): So you did. Well, that is so sweet, Michael.

MIKE: I'm making points now, huh?

J.J.: And how.

The others start pounding on the table.

MIKE: Come on, let's get this stuff on the table.

MARK: And from behind door number two, here's Carol with . . . with . . . well, it's hard to say, really.

ZONKER *stands up and brandishes the serving spoon.*

ZONKER: Back! Back! Everyone back! I'll handle this! (ZONKER *dips the spoon into the casserole. He suddenly pulls back.*) It winked. It just winked.

MIKE: Oh, for God's sake . . .

BOOPSIE: What is this dish, Mike? It certainly looks interesting.

MIKE: It's lasagne. It's my special lasagne.

He grabs the serving spoon away from ZONKER *and starts to dish the lasagne out.* B.D. *pokes at his portion with his fork.*

B.D.: Hey, Mike, where'd you get the recipe, *Sports Illustrated*?

MARK: Hey, Mike, did this stuff come in a can or did it just follow you home? You know, J.J., this is really your responsibility. You know Mike needs supervision when—

J.J.: Come on, Mark, I'm a vegetarian. I can't be held responsible for the poison that you guys—

JOANIE: You're still a vegetarian, dear?

J.J.: Oh, boy, here we go again.

MIKE: Hey! Hey! Everybody's panicking here. Now, c'mon, give me a break. Nobody's even tried the stuff yet.

MARK (*sings*):
Another memorable meal.

JOANIE (*sings*):
Spaghetti.

MARK (*sings*):
No, it's got to be veal.

ZONKER (*sings*):
Mine moved, at least it caught the light.

B.D. (*sings*):
I love a meal that picks a fight.

MARK (*sings*):
Clam Cannelloni that would make you weep.

ZONKER (*sings*):
Mike, can I have mine put to sleep?

B.D. (*sings*):
Can't hate a meatball with a lively bounce.

J.J. (*sings*):
We are proud to announce . . .

ALL (*sing*):
That it's another memorable meal.
Don't look, close your eyes and feel.
One more Michael masterpiece,
Trace your initials in the grease.

ZONKER (*sings*):
Sometimes to fight off mealtime boredom,
I like to work up a full postmortem,
Lay the little entree flat on its back,
Stuff and mount with a plaque . . .

ALL (*sing*):
Saying it's another memorable meal.

MIKE (*sings*):
Why is this such a big deal?

ALL (*sing*):
Who knows what it may conceal?

MIKE (*sings*):
Don't give a thought to how I feel.

B.D. (*sings*):
How does he get . . .

BOOPSIE and ZONKER (*sing*):
How does he get the sauce to clot?

MIKE (*sings*):
Hey, I gave it my best shot.

JOANIE (*sings*):
Now, dear, at least you served it hot.

MIKE (*sings*):
It's hot! It's hot! It's hot! It's hot!

MEN (*sing*):
Yes, it's another memorable meal.

J.J. (*sings*):
Give it time, it might congeal.

MEN (*sing*):
Top chow, with zero taste appeal.

BOOPSIE (*sings*):
It's much too weird to be real.

MEN (*sing*):
Fast food, only for the brave.
Nouveau, or maybe it's New Wave.

ALL (*sing*):
New Wave! New Wave! New Wave! New Wave!

JOANIE (*sings*):
Should this lump in the sauce be saved?

MARK and BOOPSIE (*sing*):
Sure, it's benign, it's been microwaved.

B.D. and J.J. (*sing*):
A taste sensation that will drive you to your knees.

ZONKER (*sings*):
God, it just ate my peas!

ALL (*sing*):
Another memorable meal.

BOOPSIE (*sings*):
Why make a prediction?

B.D. and BOOPSIE (*sing*):
You take your chances at the Walden Grille.

ZONKER (*sings*):
It's stranger than fiction.

ALL (*sing*):
　　Things don't turn out how you think they will.

MARK (*sings*):
　　To hear his pasta crunch is quite a thrill.

ZONKER (*sings*):
　　To stay calm while you munch, a test of skill.

B.D. (*sings*):
　　To keep from blowing lunch, a test of will.

ALL (*sing*):
　　We've had our fill,
　　We'll pass until
　　Another memorable,
　　'Nother memorable,
　　'Nother memorable,
　　Memorable meal!

As the song ends, the phone rings. ZONKER *reaches behind him and answers it.*

ZONKER: Hello? Yes, this is he. Oh, hi, Mrs. Kirby. I was going to drop by to discuss the lease with you tomorrow. We'd like to renew.

MIKE: Zonker . . .

ZONKER: What? You can't be serious. But Mrs. Kirby . . . Oh, no. Yeah, I am a little disappointed. I know. I know. Thanks for calling. Bye. (*Everyone is watching* ZONKER *as he hangs up.*) She sold it. Mrs. Kirby sold Walden.

There is stunned silence.

B.D.: Are you kidding? Who would want this dump?

In answer, a tremendous explosion blows open the front door. As the smoke clears, in walks DUKE, *clutching a teargas canister launcher. Behind him is* HONEY, *her face hidden by a gas mask.*

ZONKER: Uncle Duke!

DUKE: You people have got 24 hours to clear out of here. I've got two busloads of junkies pulling in at 0800 Tuesday.

Curtain.

ACT TWO
SCENE 1

Walden Commune. The next morning. As we open on Walden, we see
MIKE *sleeping on the living room couch. Outside the house, we hear the*
roar of an approaching bulldozer. As the din grows louder, MARK *emerges*
from his bedroom. He is wearing pajama bottoms and obviously has just
been awakened. As he staggers over to the living room window, he fails to
see MIKE *on the couch.*

MARK (*mutters to himself*): Holy Christ. What the hell is going on out
there? (*He looks out the window.*) Man, that guy doesn't waste any
time. (*As the noise becomes deafening, we see* MIKE, *still asleep, grow*
more and more agitated. He suddenly sits bolt upright and lets out a
bloodcurdling scream. MARK *nearly jumps through the window.*) Jesus!
What? What? (*As* MIKE *continues to holler,* MARK *goes over and shakes*
him by his shoulders.) Wake up! Wake up, Mike. You're dreaming. As
usual.

MIKE *finally opens his eyes and looks at* MARK *in panic.*

MIKE: Oh, God . . . Mark . . . it was . . . I was . . . God, it was awful! I
dreamed Duke was bulldozing our front yard into a parking lot.

MARK *lets go of* MIKE's *arm.*

MARK: You meatball. Duke *is* bulldozing our front yard into a parking
lot.

MIKE *listens to the noise for a moment, and then sinks back into his*
pillow.

MIKE: Oh, I get it. This is one of those dreams where you think you've woken up when in fact you're still asleep and you're just dreaming that you've woken up.

ZONKER *opens his bedroom door. He, too, has obviously just been roused.*

ZONKER (*muttering*): Boy, some people are so inconsiderate. How am I supposed to look my best for graduation? (ZONKER *shuffles past* MIKE *and* MARK *and peers out the window.*) My God. Where's the meadow?

B.D. *and* BOOPSIE *appear in their bedroom door.*

B.D.: Hey! What the hell's going on out there?

MARK: Duke's strip-mining our front lawn.

MIKE *gets up and runs to the window just as* J.J. *appears.*

J.J.: Michael? What's all the racket? It's got the baby screaming again.

MIKE *is stunned by what he sees.*

MIKE: I . . . I can't believe it. . . . There was a perfectly good meadow there. Just last night. (*To* J.J.): We walked in it. We laughed in it. We talked about the future in it.

B.D.: And I took a whiz in it. Big deal.

MIKE: B.D., you don't seem to understand what's going on here. As of tonight, Walden is no longer a commune; it's a flophouse for dopeheads and burnouts.

B.D.: Kind of a fine distinction, don't you think?

JOANIE *enters from the bedroom.*

JOANIE: Hi, guys. Everyone getting ready for the real world?

MIKE: You know, this really is the passing of an era.

B.D.: Jesus, what the hell is all the whining about? It's just a house!

MIKE, MARK, ZONKER: *Just* a house?

MIKE (*sings*):
Were the Beatles
Just a group?
Was Watergate
Just a scoop?

Was Woodstock
Merely rural?
Was Vietnam
Just intramural?
Was Marilyn . . .

ZONKER (*sings*):
  The fights, the scenes . . .

MIKE (*sings*):
  Just a shape?

ZONKER (*sings*):
  The franks, the beans . . .

MIKE (*sings*):
  Was Nixon . . .

ZONKER (*sings*):
  The laughs, the tears . . .

MIKE (*sings*):
  Just fond of tape?

ZONKER (*sings*):
  Through all those years . . .

MIKE (*sings*):
  Is the Sun Belt . . .

ZONKER (*sings*):
  When eyes would glaze . . .

MIKE (*sings*):
  Just cars and cactus?

ZONKER (*sings*):
  From killer J's . . .

MIKE (*sings*):
  Were the Falklands . . .

ZONKER (*sings*):
  On lazy days.

MIKE (*sings*):
  Target practice?

MIKE and ZONKER (*sing*):
Just a house,
Just a house,
How can you say
It's just a house?
Is Jimmy Carter . . .

MARK (*sings*):
The kegs of beer . . .

MIKE and ZONKER (*sing*):
Just a grin?

MARK (*sings*):
The nine-month year . . .

MIKE and ZONKER (*sing*):
Is nuclear war . . .

MARK (*sings*):
The happy cult . . .

MIKE and ZONKER (*sing*):
Bad for the skin?

MARK (*sings*):
The whole gestalt . . .

MIKE and ZONKER (*sing*):
Was Martha Mitchell . . .

MARK (*sings*):
The times we swore . . .

MIKE and ZONKER (*sing*):
Just a spouse?

MARK (*sings*):
A grand rapport . . .

MIKE and ZONKER (*sing*):
You ask if Walden

MARK (*sings*):
The esprit de corps.

MIKE and ZONKER (*sing*):
Is just a house.

ALL (*sing*):
  Just a house,
  Just a house,
  How can you say
  It's just a house?

At that moment, DUKE *storms through the front door. He is followed closely by* HONEY, *who is wearing a hard hat.*

DUKE: Hey! Why the hell aren't you people packing? It's moving day.

HONEY: Sir, give them a chance. They just got up.

ZONKER: Uncle Duke. We've got to talk.

DUKE: There's nothing to talk about, nephew. You people have twelve hours left.

ZONKER: Uncle Duke, you can't go ahead with this. This is our home.

DUKE: Wrong, nephew. It *was* your home. It's my place now. Anyway, what's the big deal? (*Sings.*)

  It's just a house.
  It's just a room.
  It's time to leave
  Your cozy womb.
  It's time to face
  The human race,
  It's just a place,
  And it's mine now.

ALL (*sing*):
  Just a house,
  Just a house,
  How can you say
  It's just a house?

Dance break.

ALL (*sing*):
  Was Marilyn . . .

HONEY (*sings*):
  I know how you must feel, sirs . . .

ALL (*sing*):
  Just a shape?

HONEY (*sings*):
  I really do.

ALL (*sing*):
  Was Nixon . . .

HONEY (*sings*):
  How it breaks your heart to go . . .

ALL (*sing*):
  Just fond of tape?

HONEY (*sings*):
  Start anew.

ALL (*sing*):
  Is the Sun Belt . . .

HONEY (*sings*):
  No one likes to break the tie.

ALL (*sing*):
  Just cars and cactus?

HONEY (*sings*):
  Can't deny . . .

ALL (*sing*):
  Were the Falklands . . .

HONEY (*sings*):
  No one likes to say good-bye.

ALL (*sing*):
  Target practice?
  Were the Beatles

DUKE (*sings*):
  It's just a house.

ALL (*sing*):
  Just a group?

DUKE (*sings*):
  It's just a room.

HONEY (*sings*):
  I know how you must feel,
    sirs.

HONEY (*sings*):
  I really do.

ALL (*sing*):
Was Watergate . . .

DUKE (*sings*):
It's time to leave . . .

ALL (*sing*):
Just a scoop?

DUKE (*sings*):
Your cozy womb.

ALL (*sing*):
Was Martha Mitchell . . .

DUKE (*sings*):
It's time to face . . .

ALL (*sing*):
Just a spouse?

DUKE (*sings*):
The human race.

ALL (*sing*):
Is Walden Commune . . .

DUKE (*sings*):
It's my place.

DUKE (*sings*):
But it's just a house,
Just a house,
Just a house,
Just a house!

But it's just a house,
Just a house,
Just a house,
Just a house!

HONEY (*sings*):
How it breaks your heart to
go . . .

HONEY (*sings*):
Start anew.

HONEY (*sings*):
No one likes to break the
tie . . .

HONEY (*sings*):
Can't deny . . .

HONEY (*sings*):
No one likes to say good-bye.

ALL (*sing*):
Just a house,
Just a house,
Just a house,
How can you say
It's just a house?
Just a house,
Just a house,
Just a house,
How can you say
It's just a house?

As the song ends, DUKE *looks around him.*

DUKE: You take over the evacuation, Honey. I've got to take some pictures for the brochures.

HONEY: Brochures?

DUKE: Yeah, I'd rather not use the ones from Miami again.

MIKE: Miami?

MARK: Hey, man, what's this about brochures?

DUKE: What brochures?

BOOPSIE: You just said . . .

DUKE: I most certainly did not, sweet stuff. And if you want to argue about it, stick around until tonight, when you'll be trespassing, and then you can take it up with my AK-47.

As DUKE *turns to leave the room,* B.D. *bristles and stands up.*

B.D.: Hold it right there, dork-face. Did I just hear you threaten my girlfriend?

BOOPSIE: That's okay, B.D., he—

B.D.: The hell it is. I don't care what kind of hardware he turns up with, if he comes anywhere near you, I'm going to stuff it down his throat.

DUKE'*s hand drops to his sidearm.*

DUKE: Sure you are, sonny boy.

As the two men start to square off, JOANIE *moves between them.*

JOANIE: Mr. Duke, I wonder if I might have a word with you.

B.D.: Stay out of this, Joanie.

JOANIE: Really, I must insist—

B.D.: I can handle this, Joanie!

JOANIE: Before we all lose our heads. Mr. Duke, I'm sure you're aware that a conversion of the institutional type you are proposing requires a specific ruling as to its conformity with existing zoning ordinances . . .

B.D. (*to* BOOPSIE): Great strategy. Put him to sleep.

JOANIE: So I think it's only fair to warn you that in the absence of such a ruling, my clients would be free to seek a restraining order . . .

MIKE: Clients? Did she say clients?

JOANIE: . . . as well as file a felony complaint of physical harassment.

DUKE: Wait a minute. Wait a minute, sweetheart, let me get this straight. You're actually looking to play hardball with me? (*He laughs.*) Don't make me laugh! You want to know what my favorite breakfast food is, sister? Effete ACLU looney-tune types like you!

ZONKER: Joanie! We're really your clients?

JOANIE: Well, if I can help at all, dear . . .

ZONKER (*clapping his hands*): We've got a lawyer! We've got a lawyer! Everything's going to be okay. What a relief.

He exits into his bedroom.

DUKE: Look, toots, I don't care how cheap you work, this place is legally mine now. And either all of you are out of here by tonight, or I'm going to hand you your lungs in the morning. C'mon, Honey, we've got earth to move.

DUKE *and* HONEY *exit.*

BOOPSIE: Boy, what a creep!

B.D.: Ah, the guy's basically a candy-ass.

BOOPSIE: B.D., what's an AK-47? Is that that new tape recorder with auto-reverse?

They exit.

JOANIE: Okay, guys, we better get down to the zoning office. If we're going to get an injunction in time, we'll have to move fast.

As JOANIE *runs to her room,* MIKE *goes to the couch to put on his shoes.*

MIKE: Now, this is more like it. (*To* J.J.): Isn't it amazing the difference a good authority figure can make during a crisis?

J.J.: I wouldn't know.

MIKE: Aw, c'mon, J.J., don't personalize everything. Your mother's just trying to help us save the house.

J.J.: But I thought you were moving out.

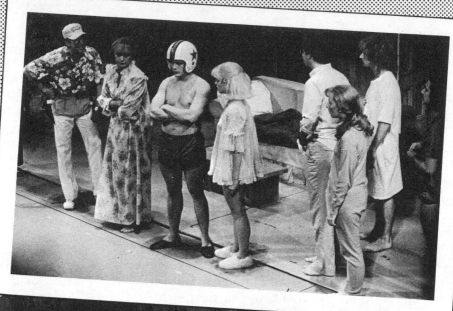

MIKE: Well, I am. But Mark and Zonker aren't. Besides, I have a lot of important memories here, J.J. (*Shouting.*) We'll bring the car around, counselor. Come on, Mark!

MARK *returns from his room. He is pulling up his pants.*

MARK: Wait a minute, Mike. Maybe we're being a little hasty here. I mean, when you think about it, what more fitting ending for Walden than a rehabilitation center? After all, Walden has always been in the business of saving people from themselves, right?

MIKE: Mark—

MARK: Wait a minute, Mike. I'm warming to my theme here.

MIKE: Your theme sucks. Come on!

MARK *sighs deeply and looks over at* J.J.

MARK: I don't know why I even bother looking at things philosophically anymore. There's just no percentage in it.

They exit. JOANIE *returns from the bedroom.*

JOANIE: J.J., would you mind watching Jeffrey for me?

J.J.: What?

JOANIE: I'd rather not take him with us. Could you keep an eye on him? I'd appreciate it.

J.J.: You want *me* to look after Jeffrey? Mother, I came that close to stuffing his pillow down his throat this morning.

JOANIE: He's quieted down now. He won't be any trouble. Please?

J.J.: Okay. He's your kid. I hope you know what you're doing.

JOANIE: Of course I know what I'm doing. I'm leaving Jeffrey with his sister.

J.J.: Don't con me, Mother. That's just a technicality.

JOANIE: All families are made up of accidents of birth, J.J. If you don't want to be his sister, you'll have to tell him yourself. I better go. Thanks.

She exits upstage right. Immediately, we hear the baby crying.

J.J.: Oh, God!

SCENE 2

The White House scrim.

REAGAN (*voice-over*): Uh . . . ladies and gentlemen, could I have your attention, please? I'd like to start by introducing two of your number, Jeff Perkins and Ken Weller, from St. George's Medical School, and Corporal Buddy Driskall, one of the Rangers who rescued them.

ALL (*voice-over*): Yea!

REAGAN (*voice-over*): Jeff, it was very easy for the media to say you were in no danger, especially since they were being protected on one of our aircraft carriers. What was it really like on Grenada?

JEFF (*voice-over*): Well, Mr. President, see, the thing of it was, there was some really bad craziness going down there, y'know? So like, we were down at the beach one morning having a few brews before Tuesday bio class, when suddenly I look up and I see all these little white spots, right? And I'm thinkin', oh, wow, the local water got me again, okay? . . .

REAGAN (*voice-over*): Thank you very much, Jeff . . .

JEFF (*voice-over*): But then I see they're really parachutes, okay? And then I'm thinkin', "Awesome, man, it's a fuckin' invasion!" . . .

REAGAN (*voice-over*): Thank you, Jeff. Why don't we hear from Ken now?

KEN (*voice-over*): Thanks, Mr. President. I just want to say I used to be a liberal, but I don't think I've ever seen a more beautiful sight than those Rangers dropping down into the pool and tennis courts. They had a job to do, and I just want to thank Buddy here and his fellow warriors.

BUDDY (*voice-over*): No sweat, man. It was a can-do situation. We went in there to kick Cuban ass, and that's what we did!

ALL (*voice-over*): Yea! We're number one! We're number one! We're number one!

SCENE 3

Walden Commune front yard. BOOPSIE *and* B.D. *are walking out to the mailbox. Offstage, we hear* DUKE's *bulldozer start up again.* BOOPSIE *looks back over her shoulder.*

BOOPSIE: Oh, no, there goes the tomato patch. I hope Joanie gets back soon.

B.D.: Who cares if she doesn't?

BOOPSIE: B.D., what is your problem? She's only trying to help.

B.D.: Help, my ass. She's taking over again. She thinks she's still our hippie-dippy housemother.

BOOPSIE: Well, I think she's being very nice. Besides, what difference does it make to you? I thought you didn't care about what happened to Walden.

B.D.: I don't.

BOOPSIE: Yes, you do. Now, c'mon, B.D., admit it, you're going to miss the place. And you'll miss the guys.

B.D.: Give me a break, Boopsie.

BOOPSIE: B.D., do you remember that discussion we had about not being afraid of your feelings?

B.D.: Vividly.

BOOPSIE: And remember you said you'd try to be more honest about your emotions during the off-season?

BOOPSIE *reaches into the mailbox and pulls out the mail.*

B.D.: Come on, Boopsie, that was before the draft. I'm a professional athlete now. What's that?

BOOPSIE: It's a mailgram. It's for you. (*She pulls it out.*) From Sid Kibitz. Who's he?

B.D.: My agent. (*He takes the mailgram from* BOOPSIE *and starts to read it.*) Oh, no . . .

BOOPSIE: What is it, B.D.?

B.D. *doesn't answer but continues reading with a pained expression.*

B.D.: Goddamn son of a bitch!

He crumples the mailgram and hurls it to the ground. BOOPSIE *picks it up and starts to read it.*

BOOPSIE: "Sorry to inform you Cowboys have traded you to Tampa Bay Buccaneers for two draft picks and a bus. Dallas' loss is Tampa's gain. Be cool, babe. Who loves you? Sid."

B.D.: A bus. I got my ass traded for a goddamn bus.

BOOPSIE: Maybe they really needed one, B.D. You know, to get their players out to practice. Their old one probably broke down and . . . (B.D. *gives* BOOPSIE *a withering look.*) Oh, B.D., you're still going to be playing football. What's the difference if you do it for the Cowboys or the Buccaneers?

B.D.: About forty grand and a ring the size of a grapefruit.

BOOPSIE: B.D., the important thing is that we can still be together. I'll just try out for the Tampettes! (*When* B.D. *says nothing,* BOOPSIE *starts to look concerned.*) B.D.? Baby, are you okay? B.D.? You're not crying, are you? (B.D. *slowly looks up. He's not even close to crying.*) It's okay, baby. Let it all out.

B.D.: Let what out?

BOOPSIE: Really. There's nothing unmanly about crying. Remember that Donahue show? The one on male growthfulness?

B.D.: Boopsie!

Unseen by both B.D. *and* BOOPSIE, HONEY *has entered.*

HONEY: Excuse me, sir and miss. (BOOPSIE *and* B.D. *look up.*) Are you finished with the mailbox? Mr. Duke has asked me to take it down.

B.D. *walks over to the mailbox and with one violent jerk yanks it out of the ground. He hands it to an awe-stricken* HONEY.

HONEY: Wow!

B.D.: Let me know if he has any trouble deciding what to do with it.

HONEY: If I may say so, sir, that was a rather impressive physical feat. You're quite a specimen.

BOOPSIE: C'mon, baby, let's talk it out.

B.D.: Boopsie, will you get off that? There's nothing to talk out, for Christ's sake. I got traded to Tampa Bay. Period. And I don't need Phil Donahue to tell me why I am pissed off!

B.D. *exits.*

BOOPSIE: There's a lot of pain there. A lot of denial. What am I going to do?

HONEY: I don't know, miss. I've never been involved with a thoroughbred. When Mr. Duke gets upset, I usually just change his medication.

BOOPSIE: Men are so funny, you know? Whenever they have a crisis, they just bottle it all up inside. Why do we put up with it?

HONEY: Well, personally, miss, I don't have any choice. Greatness has a narcotic effect on me. I'm attracted to it. I like to date it. But sometimes there's a price to pay. A man like Mr. Duke has to be handled very carefully. (*Sings.*)

He's a complicated man.
So full of contradictions,
I hold back all I can.
While I cannot make predictions,
I know he'd have a plan.
First he'd ask for sympathy,
Then he'd want his way with me,
This complicated man.
He's a complicated man,
We knew it would be difficult
Back when our love began.
How many nights he's had to toss
Alone beneath the fan.
Though his carnal needs run deep,
Living legends need their sleep.
This complicated man.

BOOPSIE: Oh, I know just how you feel, Honey. My guy's a handful, too. (*Sings.*)

He's a complicated man,
He always has distractions,
So I grab him when I can.
No other girl has understood
His short attention span.
Although he's usually hot to go,
A quarterback can underthrow.
My complicated man.

BOTH (*sing*):
And when the day breaks,
I wake him up and start his heart . . .

BOOPSIE (*sings*):
With chocolate pancakes . . .

HONEY (*sings*):
And dexedrine . . .

BOTH (*sing*):
I do my part
To make him feel he's a star.
I do not make assumptions,
I worship him from afar.
And though he seems to look through me,
I have his full fidelity,
It's just that he was born to be
A complicated man.
He's a complicated man.
No time for false humility,
He's always running late.
It's my responsibility
To make sure that he's straight.

BOOPSIE (*sings*):
A shoulder to revive on . . .

HONEY (*sings*):
And rest his .45 on . . .

BOTH (*sing*):
This complicated man.
And when the sun sets,
We cuddle up and spend the night . . .

BOOPSIE (*sings*):
With T.V. wrestling . . .

HONEY (*sings*):
And nudie flicks . . .

BOTH (*sing*):
In black and white.
I make him feel he's a star.
I do not make assumptions,
I worship him from afar.
And though he seems to look through me,
I have his full fidelity,
It's just that he was born to be
A complicated man.
A complicated man,
I'm his biggest fan,
This complicated man.

SCENE 4

Walden Puddle. ZONKER *is snorkling in Walden Puddle when* DUKE *enters.*

DUKE: Oh, Christ, where's the corner marker? I don't believe this. She had all night to get them in. (*He looks around him.*) God almighty. Sometimes Honey truly amazes me. The woman cannot perform the simplest task.

ZONKER: Uncle Duke, what are you doing?

DUKE: Triangulating. At least I'm trying to. You better get out of that pond, nephew. I'm going to be filling it in in a few minutes.

ZONKER: You *what?*

DUKE: It's in the way. I gotta squeeze four tennis courts in between the house and the property line.

ZONKER: Tennis courts? For junkies? Uncle Duke, something stinks here. I don't know what you're up to, but there are some things family friends don't do to one another. If you go through with this—

DUKE: Okay, okay. We are family, Zonker, so I'm going to level with you. I have no intention of turning a property this magnificent into a re-hab center. No, I've got bigger plans, nephew, plans to turn Walden into the priciest, most profitable vacation condo complex in New England.

ZONKER: Condos. You just said condos.

DUKE: I sure did. How would you like a job?

ZONKER: Uncle Duke, there is nothing having to do with condos that could possibly make me consider accepting a—

DUKE: I'd like you to be my resident tanning director.

ZONKER: I could start Monday.

DUKE: There you go. You won't regret it, boy. It's time you joined the '80s. Real estate is ringing everyone's bell these days. (*Sings.*)

Condo,
Mondo condo.
Mondo condo and I buy me a home.
Real estate.
Real estate.
Real estate.
Real estate.
Picked up my phone, called my broker.
Asked about my latest deal.
Mondo condo sure beats poker,
So obscene that it's surreal . . .
Estate.

ALL:
Real estate.
Real estate.
Real estate.
Real estate.

ZONKER (*sings*):
Is it easy?

DUKE (*sings*):
Hard to hate.

ZONKER (*sings*):
Is it sleazy?

DUKE (*sings*):
Just partake.

ZONKER (*sings*):
Can I hack it?

DUKE (*sings*):
Piece of cake.

ZONKER (*sings*):
What a racket.

DUKE (*sings*):
It's pure gold to renovate
Residentials, but, boy, I hate
Pushing poor folks back
    uptown.
They'll take anything that's
    not nailed down.

BACKUP VOCALISTS:
Laka-laka-Kiko-Seka
Gio-a-Ci-Si-Ba-Ow-I
Back, back, back uptown.

ZONKER (*sings*):
   Just vacate?

DUKE (*sings*):
   Get 'em off it.

ZONKER (*sings*):
   Confiscate?

DUKE (*sings*):
   Net a profit.

ZONKER (*sings*):
   Renovate?

DUKE (*sings*):
   Fix the entry.

ZONKER (*sings*):
   Real estate!

DUKE (*sings*):
   For the gentry.
   Picked up the phone, I had an inkling,
   Scored some condo, what a steal,
   Turned it over in a twinkling,
   It's too wild to be for real . . .
   Estate.
   Just conduct it.

ZONKER (*sings*):
   Interest rate?

DUKE (*sings*):
   Just deduct it.

ZONKER (*sings*):
   Fabricate.

DUKE (*sings*):
   Sixty units.

ZONKER (*sings*):
   Celebrate.

DUKE (*sings*):
   Sing the tune, it's . . .

DUKE (*sings*):
Great, dear protégé,
Folks don't judge you the same today.
You buy a new home, they don't care how,
Just what you paid and what it goes for now . . .
A-days.
Bailar!

Dance break.

BACKUP VOCALISTS:
Aah
Laka-laka-Kiko-Seka
Aah
Gio-a-Ci-Si-Ba-Ow-I
Aah
No, no, no, no,
They don't care how!

DUKE (*sings*):
Just what you paid and what it goes for nowadays.

ZONKER (*sings*):
It's the answer?

DUKE (*sings*):
Yeah, it pays.

ZONKER (*sings*):
Can I tan, sir?

DUKE (*sings*):
Private decks!

ZONKER (*sings*):
On the sun side?

DUKE (*sings*):
Sure beats sex.

ZONKER (*sings*):
On the fun side.

BOTH (*sing*):
Mondo condo, here we come!
Mondo condo (etc.)

ZONKER: Tan, tan, tan!

SCENE 5

Walden Commune. An hour later. J.J. *is on the sofa with the baby when* MIKE *enters. He heads immediately for the kitchen.*

MIKE: Hi, J.J. Sorry I'm late.

J.J.: Oh, hi, Mike. Late for what?

MIKE: Our 9:40 breakfast, of course. Didn't you read today's schedule? (MIKE *is rushing frantically around the kitchen, grabbing the ingredients for a makeshift breakfast.*) If we skip the grapefruit, maybe we can make up the time. I'm really sorry. We got hung up at the zoning office. But we've got Duke cold. We notified the sheriff's office. Joanie's outside now reading him the riot act. (*He walks out of the kitchen with a tray laden with two glasses of orange juice and a plate of doughnuts.*) Hope you don't mind doughnuts and O.J. I could make some eggs if you— (*He notices two empty cereal bowls on the coffee table.*) Hey, J.J., you've already eaten.

J.J.: Huh? Oh, yeah, I guess I have. I'm sorry, Michael. The kid and I got hungry, so we had some Grape-Nuts.

MIKE: Grape-Nuts? You gave Grape-Nuts to a six-month-old baby? J.J., he doesn't even have any teeth yet.

J.J.: I know. It wasn't easy getting them down. He was a real champ though. He only spit up a couple.

MIKE *looks at the baby.*

MIKE: Uh . . . J.J.?

J.J.: What?

MIKE: You've . . . you've drawn a mustache on him.

J.J.: Yeah. Don't you think it makes him look distinguished?

MIKE *reaches for a napkin.*

MIKE: Come on, we better get that stuff off. I don't think Joanie will be very pleased to find out you've been defacing her baby.

J.J. *pulls the baby away.*

J.J.: Hey! Leave him alone. He's my brother. I can do whatever I want with him.

MIKE: You're just doing this to get at Joanie, aren't you?

J.J.: Hey, c'mon, Michael. Whose side are you on, anyway?

MIKE: Why do I have to be on someone's side? Why do there have to be sides?

J.J.: What can I tell you, Michael. It happens.

MIKE: It does not. It only happens if you let it. And you're letting it. You think just because of something your mother did a long time ago that you've got some kind of permanent claim to the moral high ground, that you're somehow entitled to punish her for the rest of her life. Well, what are you getting from that, J.J.? Satisfaction? You're getting nothing. And you're missing everything. And it makes me angry as hell, because I care about you, and there's nothing I can do to change things. That's up to you, but you're so damn busy taking it out on the baby, you can't see how hard Joanie's trying to get you back.

J.J. *looks at* MIKE *with astonishment.*

J.J.: Michael?

MIKE: What?

J.J.: Did you write that out?

MIKE: No, I didn't write that out. I mean, what do you think? I don't always write everything out. J.J., didn't you hear a word I said?

J.J.: Yes, I did. I heard every word you said. I love you. (MIKE *is totally disarmed. He starts to embrace* J.J. *when he glances at his watch.*)

MIKE: Oh, God. I have to go get dressed for graduation.

He exits into his bedroom. J.J., *clearly disappointed, returns to the sofa.* JOANIE *enters, brushing dust from her skirt. She appears very agitated.*

JOANIE: That man is amazing. I've never seen such perfect arrogance. He just laughed at the restraining order. All he wanted to know was what the firepower of the local police was. How do you reason with someone like that? (JOANIE *walks over to the couch*.) So. How'd you two get along? He's not such a bad little guy, is he? I just have a feeling that once you get to know him, you'll . . . (*She takes a closer look at* JEFFREY.) What's that on his face? Is that supposed to be a mustache? J.J., have you been drawing graffiti on your brother? (JOANIE *smiles*.) Actually, it's quite becoming. It makes his face look rather . . . distinguished, wouldn't you say? Yes, it's a definite improvement. So. Want me to take him off your hands now? Honey?

J.J. *is still looking at the baby as she answers.*

J.J.: No, it's all right, Mom. I've got him. I mean, if that's okay with you.

JOANIE: Okay with me? You can't imagine how okay that is with me.

J.J.: Listen, Mom, I fed him breakfast, okay? The baby stuff you bought yesterday had sugar and preservatives in it, so I gave him some Grape-Nuts instead. It's really important that you feed him the right food, Mom. I could give you some books on it.

JOANIE *smiles.*

JOANIE: J.J.?

J.J.: Yes, Mom?

JOANIE: You've really become quite lovely, you know.

J.J. (*surprised*): Thanks, Mom.

JOANIE (*sings*):
Just to feel what I feel when I look in her eyes,
Where was I when I first saw that look,
Heard those cries?
It was strange to be her mother
And not know how to love,
How hard to be her friend now that I do.
Baby, I never stopped missing you.

J.J. (*sings*):
Just to feel what I feel when I look at her pride,
How I missed all he has, how I held it inside.

It was strange to be a daughter
And not know a mother's love,
How hard to be her friend now that I do.
Mother, I never stopped missing you.

JOANIE (*sings*):
   All those years that I tried to be your mother
   I had dreams,
   A kind of madness.

J.J. (*sings*):
   All my fears it was not enough to love you
   They came true,
   I felt your sadness.

BOTH (*sing*):
   Can we ever find the love together
   That we lost while learning how to fly?

J.J. (*sings*):
   Can I reach you again?
   Maybe I can try.

JOANIE: You mean it, honey?

J.J.: Yeah. Maybe there should be a statute of limitations on this thing.
   It's like in that Pat Benatar song, you know, the one she did that video
   on with the leopards and the sand dunes . . . ?

   JOANIE *laughs*.

JOANIE: I guess I didn't see that one. You like that stuff, do you?

J.J.: Sure. It's okay.

JOANIE: I can't tell you how much I've missed interfering in your life.

J.J.: Me, too, Mom.

BOTH (*sing*):
   Can we ever find the love together
   That we lost while learning how to fly?
   Can I reach you again?

JOANIE (*sings*):
   Maybe I . . .

J.J. (*sings*):
　Maybe I . . .

BOTH (*sing*):
　Maybe I can try.
　Just to feel what I'd feel if I had you again.
　There were times when I felt
　That the pain wouldn't end.
　And how hard it was to love you
　When I never had you near,
　How strange to be your friend now that I do.

J.J. (*sings*):
　Mother . . .

JOANIE (*sings*):
　Baby . . .

BOTH (*sing*):
　I'll never let go of you.

　As the song ends, ROLAND *appears at the door.*

ROLAND: Hello? Roland Hedley here. ABC. Don't worry if you're not decent. I'm sans camera crew. (*He walks in and takes out his notebook.*) You must be proud family members.

　MIKE *enters from his room. He has shaving cream on his face and a towel around his neck.*

MIKE: Roland? What are you doing here?

ROLAND: The graduation interviews, son. Did you forget? We've been set up on the quad for an hour.

JOANIE: Oh, dear, is it getting that late? I better hurry or we won't get any good seats. J.J., will you make sure Mike doesn't miss his own graduation?

　MIKE *hands* JOANIE *her jacket and the diaper bag, and she exits carrying the baby.*

MIKE: You'll have to excuse us, Roland. Things have been real crazy around here, and—

ROLAND: That's why I'm in town, lad. To capture some of those hijinks on tape and share them with my viewers.

MARK *enters through the front door.*

MARK: Roland!

ROLAND: Marvelous Mark! Congratulations, son.

MARK: Thanks, Roland, but it's no big deal. For $40,000, they have to give you a diploma.

ROLAND: No, I mean about your new job. I stopped by to see your station manager this morning, you know, to put in a good word—

MARK: And he loved the show last night?

ROLAND: No, actually, he missed it. But as Lady Luck would have it, one of the veeps for the chain that owns the station was listening in, and he wants to put you on the air in New York.

MARK (*stunned*): He what?

MIKE: New York? Mark got a job in New York?

ROLAND: Well, Long Island, actually. But it's your kind of station—an all-talk format with a tiny, devoted audience. It's practically public radio.

MIKE: Good going, Mark. That's great.

MARK: This is absolutely amazing, Mike. My life is coming together!

ROLAND: I wonder if you could put a cap on some of that enthusiasm, youngsters. I'd like to get your filmed reaction once you're suited up.

MARK: Suited up? Oh, you mean the . . . gowns! My God, Mike, we forgot to pick up the gowns.

MIKE: Oh, no . . .

ROLAND *laughs as* B.D. *and* BOOPSIE *enter. They are carrying five caps and gowns.*

ROLAND: Love it. Forgot the gowns. I'm going to have to work that in. Funny bit.

B.D.: Relax, kiddies. At least somebody was doing something useful this morning.

MARK: Hey, good save, Captain America.

MARK *and* MIKE *both get their gowns from* B.D. MIKE *and* J.J. *return to his room.*

BOOPSIE: Hi, Rollie. Long time, no see.

ROLAND: Too long, young lady.

MARK *goes to* ZONKER's *door to give him his gown.*

MARK: Zonker!

ZONKER *opens his door.*

ZONKER: What? Aiee!

He grabs the gown and slams the door. MARK *exits into his own room.*

ROLAND (*to* B.D.): I guess congratulations are in order for you, too, son.

B.D.: You talkin' to me?

ROLAND: I hear you were traded to Tampa Bay.

B.D.: That's what you heard, huh?

ROLAND: The Buccaneers, huh? Shrewd move. In Dallas, you'd just be sitting around praying for Danny White's knees to crack. In Tampa Bay, on the other hand, I daresay you'll be a demigod.

BOOPSIE: A demigod! Hear that, B.D.? (*Getting up.*) I gotta go put my face on. Won't be long.

BOOPSIE *heads back for the bedroom. She stops for a second and looks proudly back at* B.D.

BOOPSIE: A demigod. I could just die!

BOOPSIE *exits.*

ROLAND: Pretty heady stuff for a kid right out of college. I'm guessing you'll be making quite a fair piece of change.

B.D.: You better believe it.

ROLAND: Well, that counts for something these days, son. There's a whole new ballgame in town. It's called "making it," and we've got the Big Gip to thank for bringing it all back in style. If he's done nothing else, the President has made it fun to be rich again.

B.D.: Well, what's the point otherwise?

B.D.: Fifty years of liberal guilt is enough. (*Sings.*)
Those ghetto types got all the breaks,
Rent control and food stamp steaks,

Time we closed that welfare zoo
Where ne'er-do-wells are well-to-do.

ROLAND (*sings*):
Give it back to those folks which
Had the good sense to be rich,
Folks who aren't ashamed to say,
"I've got bucks and I'm okay."

BOTH (*sing*):
It's the right time to be rich,
Yes, it's the right time to make the switch.
What you leave on your plate
Would feed a family of eight,
You only have the best.
Goodwill will pick up the rest.
It's the right time to have a buck,
It's a bad time to drive a truck,
And you're not to blame
For just playin' the game,
As long as you don't perform real work,
You're allowed to go berserk.
It's the right time to take pains
Not to pay on capital gains.
The guy who loads the dice
On his broker's advice,
He's where the buck should stop,
The lonely guy at the top.
The right time to reminisce
About those class lines we sorely miss,
It's a fine time to sing old melodies
Of those good times when we took our ease.

B.D.: Ladies and gentlemen . . .

ROLAND: Muffy and the Topsiders!

BOOPSIE, MIKE, MARK, *and* ZONKER *enter bedecked in full preppy regalia.*

BOOPSIE (*sings*):
I was a poor teenaged preppy, pink yarn in my hair,
I played field hockey and learned to kiss air.

My mummy told me, "Darling, lead with your chin,
You can't be too rich or too thin."
When you're a preppy, you keep your skin clear,
With sun every weekend and sex once a year.
I love Fancy Nancy, I love Ronnie, too.
What a pity their money is so new.

ALL (*sing*):
It's a good time to be rich,
It's a good time to scratch that itch.
And what do you care
If you dirty the air?
Palm Springs is always clean.
I'll meet you on the third green.
It's a bad time for the dole,
When the rich are on a roll.
When the good times hit a fever pitch,
It's the right time,
It's the right time,
It's the right time to be rich.

BOOPSIE, MIKE, MARK, *and* ZONKER *exit.* ROLAND *turns to* B.D.

ROLAND: Well, lad, time for your date with destiny. Can I give you a lift in my limo?

B.D.: Limo? Boopsie! Come on! We're riding to graduation in a limo!

BOOPSIE *appears at her bedroom door.*

BOOPSIE: A limo? I can't stand it!

ROLAND (*chuckling*): All aboard.

ROLAND *exits with* B.D. *and* BOOPSIE. ZONKER *enters from his bedroom. He is wearing his gown.*

ZONKER: Mike? Mark?

MIKE, MARK, *and* J.J. *enter.*

MARK: What is it, Z?

ZONKER: Gentlemen, I have what I'm confident you'll agree is electrifying news. There's been a breakthrough. I have found full employment.

MIKE and MARK: What!

ZONKER: Uncle Duke has asked me to be his tanning director. Right here at Walden Estates. It's supposed to be a secret but—

MIKE: Walden what?

MARK: Condos. I knew it.

MIKE: He doesn't mean condos, Mark. You don't mean condos, do you, Zonker?

ZONKER: Mike, try to understand. My ship has come in. It's emotionally satisfying work, the hours are good, I get discounts at the pro shop . . .

MARK: Yeah, but condos?

MIKE: Zonker, he's bought you off. He's thrown you a bone to get your cooperation.

Outside the house, the bulldozer has started up again, and we hear it approach.

ZONKER: A bone? You call tanning director of one of the most prestigious vacation complexes in New England a bone? I can't believe my ears. For the love of Mike, I've been given a remarkable opportunity here . . . (*Outside, the din grows louder and louder.*) Don't you see, guys, I can stay here and build a life for myself. I can find my place in the sun . . .

The roar has become deafening. As the four turn around to see what's happening, there is a terrible crash, and DUKE *blasts his way into the living room with the bulldozer. The boys scatter, and* J.J. *screams and dives down behind the couch. As the dust clears,* HONEY *steps in through what's left of the front door.* DUKE *surveys the wreckage around him.*

DUKE: Well, shit.

ZONKER: On the other hand, who wants to work for a complete slime-bag?

DUKE: Goddammit. That does it. I'm changing pharmacologists.

HONEY: I thought you were just going to clear out the hedges, sir.

DUKE *hops down from the bulldozer cab onto the back of the sofa.*

DUKE: Used to be a time when you knew what went into that stuff. I need

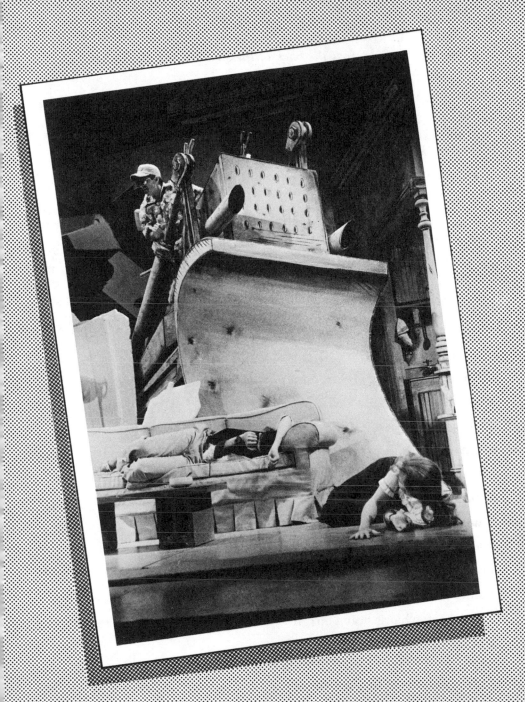

a beer. (*He walks across the back of the sofa toward the kitchen.*) Hey, don't get up.

HONEY: You've really made a mess this time, sir. I'd better go get the tool kit.

HONEY *exits.* DUKE *takes a beer out of the refrigerator and slumps down onto the kitchen floor.* MARK *looks up at the bulldozer.*

MARK: Isn't this just turning out to be the nuttiest day?

J.J. *gets up off the floor.*

J.J.: You know, this place is really beginning to get on my nerves. Michael, can we just . . . Michael? Hey, are you okay?

MIKE: Me? Sure, I'm fine. Never better. A stoned madman nearly just killed all of us, but these things happen, you know? The question is, why do they always happen to me? This was supposed to be the most important day of my life. Nothing could spoil it. I was graduating. I was getting engaged. I was—

J.J.: Engaged!

MIKE *looks at* J.J. *and then buries his face in his hands.*

MIKE: Oh . . . God . . .

J.J.: *Engaged!*

ZONKER: That was exactly my reaction. I couldn't believe it, either.

MARK: Take your time, Mike. We'll be waiting outside.

ZONKER: We will?

MARK *collars* ZONKER *and pulls him toward the door.*

MARK: Hope you make it to section B, buddy.

MIKE: Section B? (*Under his breath.*) Oh, no . . . my proposal.

MIKE *runs over to the T.V. stand and starts searching for his outline.*

J.J.: Michael, what is going on? Are you really going to ask me to marry you?

MIKE: Uh, yeah, but I . . . I need to find my notes.

J.J.: No, you don't. Just ask me.

MIKE *stops going through his papers and looks over at* J.J. *As* J.J. *waits demurely,* MIKE *slowly walks over to her. He drops to one knee.*

MIKE: J.J.? Hi. It's me, Mike.

J.J. *rolls her eyes.*

J.J.: Oh, for God's sake . . .

MIKE: J.J., will you marry me? (*When* J.J. *hesitates in responding,* MIKE *has a sudden failure of confidence.*) I don't need your answer right away. Think about it. Take the summer. I know you want to go to art school and—

J.J.: Michael, are you sure? Do you really think we're ready for this? I mean, we haven't even slept together yet.

MIKE: That was going to be my second question.

J.J.: Well, it's about time.

MIKE *stares at* J.J. *in disbelief.*

MIKE: Uh . . . yeah, I know, but it just seemed like such a big step, you know, and I just didn't . . . I mean, I wasn't sure if . . .

A delightful suspicion begins to dawn on J.J.

J.J.: Michael?

MIKE: What?

J.J.: You've never done it, have you?

MIKE: Done it? (MIKE *looks down at his hands.*) Uh . . . no.

J.J. *looks at* MIKE *with all the excitement of an eight-year-old who has just met someone who has never seen* Star Wars.

J.J.: Hey?

MIKE *looks up nervously.*

MIKE: What?

J.J.: You're going to love it. It's great. It's *really* great. Oh, God, I can't wait!

MIKE: Yeah?

J.J.: You really mean it? You really want to make love to me?

MIKE *slowly turns toward the audience.*

MIKE (*sings*):
   Just one night,
   I could be wrong about how long it's best to wait.
   Just one night,
   I'd hate to change my mind and find that I'm too late.

MIKE and J.J. (*sing*):
   I know we're new at learning how to care,
   But if you come to me
   A night that's sweet and silvery,

MIKE (*sings*):
   I'll know that I was right.

MIKE and J.J. (*sing*):
   Love is more
   Than something for
   Just one night.

   As J.J. *and* MIKE *exit, we hear a groan from the kitchen.*

DUKE: Oh, Jesus. Here come the bats. (DUKE *crawls to his feet. He grabs a spatula and starts flailing at the air.*) My God. They're all wearing . . . panty hose.

   HONEY *enters, carrying the tool kit.*

HONEY: Sir? Were you expecting company?

DUKE (*bellowing*): You don't have to scream, Honey! Oh, Christ, it's getting dark again. What keeps blotting out the sun? Aunt Helga! So we meet again, O foulest of she-devils! (*Brandishing spatula.*) Prepare to suck steel!

HONEY: It looks like it might be the authorities, sir.

DUKE: The authorities! Mother of God! We're in for a siege. Give me the tools, Honey!

   HONEY *hands him the tool kit.*

HONEY: What sort of siege, sir?

DUKE: A firefight, Honey. God knows what some of these local storm troopers are capable of.

DUKE: Get the AK-47 out of the pickup! No! Take a position in the up-stairs bathroom! No, no! Go around back and hit their right flank! Three 4-inch mortar rounds, evenly spaced, thirty seconds apart . . . when . . . I . . . (DUKE *looks at* HONEY *and squints*.) Honey, is that you?

HONEY: Yes, sir. It's me.

DUKE: You . . . you look different.

HONEY: I had my hair cut last week, sir. That may be throwing you.

DUKE: I've . . . I've never seen such beautiful antlers in my entire life.

DUKE *falls face-first into the couch.* HONEY *looks at* DUKE *and shakes her head ruefully.*

HONEY: Sir, I'm worried about your mood swings.

SCENE 6

Campus. Graduation. An hour later. The PROVOST *is in the middle of the stage preparing to hand out diplomas. In front of him to the left, seated on folding chairs, are* JOANIE *and* J.J. *To the right of the* PRESIDENT, *waiting for their diplomas, are* B.D., MIKE, MARK, BOOPSIE, *and* ZONKER. *On the far left of the stage,* ROLAND *is doing a standup report on the proceedings.*

ROLAND: And that would appear to be the conclusion of the President's commencement address to the Class of 1983. For those of you who have just joined us, the President began his remarks with . . . let's see . . . a salutation, followed by several platitudes and some pontification, apparently a rehash of what he said last year. He then squeezed off a wry joke which the students seemed to enjoy very much, and continued with two sweeping statements, a dramatic pause which this reporter found . . . very effective, and wrapped it up with a call for action. The address completed, the Provost is now preparing to confer degrees on the graduating seniors. We'll be back with more live NCAA commencement coverage after this.

ZONKER: You really think Uncle Duke's okay, Mike?

MIKE: I'm sure he's fine, Zonker. We didn't hear any gunfire. The important thing is you're going to get your house back.

ZONKER: What do you mean, my house? You're not backing out on me, are you?

MIKE: Well, Zonk, I've talked it over with J.J., and we've agreed maybe it's time to move on.

ZONKER: Whatever for?

MIKE: Well, so we could have a place of our own.

ZONKER: Whatever for?

MIKE: Uh, well, there's a . . . a kind of project we want to work on this summer.

ZONKER: Project? A project. Can you believe that?

MARK: A man's got to do what he's got to do, Zonker. Especially if he's never done it before.

ZONKER: Yeah, but how could he do it to *us*?

MARK: Actually, Zonk, I'm afraid I'm going to have to move on, too. I got a job.

ZONKER: What!

MARK: Talk radio show in New York. I can't turn it down, man. It's what I want to do.

ZONKER *stares at* MARK *with a look of complete betrayal. He shakes his head sadly.*

ZONKER: Et tu, Marcus.

ROLAND: We're back. The Provost is now about to announce the names of the graduating seniors. Let's pick up the action live.

PRESIDENT: Barbara Ann Boopstein.

ROLAND (*whispering into microphone*): Barbara Ann Boopstein.

MARK: Come on, Zonk, don't be like that. You don't need us, ol' buddy. There'll be a new generation of students coming into Walden.

PRESIDENT: B. John Dowling.

ROLAND (*whispering*): B. John Dowling.

MIKE: Yeah, Zonk, and they'll be looking to you for leadership and inspiration.

B.D.: Go Delta Kaps!

ZONKER: I don't want to be the house hippie. I'm too old for that. Please, you guys, don't do this.

MIKE and MARK: Courage.

PRESIDENT: Michael James Doonesbury, cum laude.

J.J.: Yea, Michael!

ROLAND (*whispering*): Michael James Doonesbury, cum laude.

MARK: Cum laude? Mike, you weenie!

PRESIDENT: Mark Sheldon Slackmeyer.

ROLAND (*whispering*): Mark Sheldon Slackmeyer.

MARK *goes up to receive his diploma, leaving* ZONKER *by himself. As* MIKE *comes down the other side of the stage, he is greeted by* JOANIE *and* J.J. JOANIE *has a flash camera.*

JOANIE: Michael! Over here, with J.J. I want a picture of the two love-birds.

J.J.: Lovers, Mom. We're lovers.

As J.J. *puts her arm around* MIKE, MARK *descends the platform and jumps into the picture.*

PRESIDENT: Edgar Zonker Harris.

ROLAND (*whispering*): Edgar Zonker Harris.

MARK: Edgar?

ZONKER *remains frozen in place. The others wave to him.*

MIKE: Come on, Zonk. Nothing to it.

BOOPSIE: You can do it, Zonk.

ZONKER *still doesn't move. He begins to twitch.*

PRESIDENT: Edgar Zonker Harris.

ROLAND (*whispering*): Edgar Zonker Harris.

MARK: Edgar! Get up there!

MIKE (*to* MARK): Come on. He's clutching.

MIKE *and* MARK *run over to* ZONKER, *grab him, and start walking him up the steps.*

ZONKER: No, no, I'm not ready.

MIKE: You're as ready as you'll ever be, Zonker.

ZONKER: But I don't deserve it. I don't know anything. I can't even remember my major. No, please, I need more time. This isn't fair. *I'm not ready!*

MIKE *holds up* ZONKER's *arm. As* ZONKER *cringes, the* PROVOST *stuffs his diploma into his hand.*

ROLAND:
That's the view here
For the time being.
All that's clear, Sam,
Remains to be seen
Whether or not, Ted,
This outlook survives,
Time will tell what
We do with our lives.

THE COMPANY *sings the lyric in echo as* ROLAND *speaks it.*

ALL (*sing*):
Graduation
  (Strange as it seems)
Will probably stand
  (End of our dreams)
The test of time
  (Dreams we forsake)
And it's almost at hand.
  (To go on the make)
Whether we sort
  (Go with the flow)
The pros from the con,
  (Win, place, or show)
Time will tell
If life will go on.

THE COMPANY *settles on the graduation dais in photo formation as the curtain falls.*